MW01096973

Project Management Skills for Instructional Designers

A Practical Guide

Dorcas M. T. Cox

iUniverse, Inc.
New York   Bloomington

Project Management Skills for Instructional Designers
A Practical Guide

iUniverse books may be ordered through booksellers or by contacting:

iUniverse
1663 Liberty Drive
Bloomington, IN 47403
www.iuniverse.com
1-800-Authors (1-800-288-4677)

ISBN: 978-1-4401-9363-7 (pbk)
ISBN: 978-1-4401-9365-1 (cloth)
ISBN: 978-1-4401-9364-4 (ebk)

Library of Congress Control Number: 2009912949

Printed in the United States of America

iUniverse rev. date: 12/30/2009

Cover Design by Dr. Desiree Cox

To my mother, my sister, and my son

Contents

Preface

I have worked as a practitioner in the human resources profession for more than fourteen years, as a human resources manager and more recently as an instructional designer. In 2008, I earned my PMP (Project Management Professional) designation from the Project Management Institute (PMI).

Prior to earning my PMP, my approach to projects as an instructional designer was random. While I had skills in instructional-systems design, I had no structured method for project execution, which resulted in wasted time, false starts, and untold frustration for me and the team I managed. I found that having the knowledge in instructional design is not enough when the mandate is to use instructional design skills in the context of a project. The additional knowledge and skill in project management is essential. Prior to earning my PMP, I searched for and read several books on project management for people in the human resources and training profession. While these books were good, none of them actually married the instructional-systems design and project-management disciplines in a way that I understood. Also, I needed more visual samples and templates that I could use right away in my work setting. Hopefully, my book captures the components that I sought and may provide additional insight to readers for their performance improvement.

Acknowledgments

There are so many people who have assisted in my career development to whom I owe the success of this book. I begin by thanking the many people who have managed my professional development throughout my career: Bernice Francis, Janeen McCartney, Kenneth N. Francis, Shereece Saunders, Opal Bastian, Myrna Wilson, Wayde Christie, Minna Israel, Joan Griffin, Stephanie Doberstein, and Joanna Bowe. Collectively, you have taught me what to do and what not to do to survive in the corporate world. Without you, I would not be where I am today.

To Carmen Trejo, Carla Serrano, Carolina Perez, Maureen Wallace, Elizabeth (Liz) Burrows, Audette Sheppard, Adrian Strachan, Anthony Allens, Theo Tsavoussis, Donna Delancy and Stephen Ash, who helped me through a very difficult period and gave me the support, strength, and courage that I needed to continue trying. Thank you. Special thanks to Marvin Clarke, who introduced me to project management, and to Tim Rudkins and Kola Osisanwo, who helped me to see it through to the end.

I owe a depth of gratitude to my mother, Ena-Mae T. Cox, who taught me instructional design and how to write task lists as a little girl, and who supported me in developing facilitation skills. I thank you for your love, support, and encouragement. Without these contributions, none of this would be possible. To Dr. Kirkland Culmer, my surrogate dad, uncle Albert Ferguson and my long time friends Stephan Edgecombe, Renee McKinney, and Vernique Thompson who have always and continue to support and encourage me along the way. Special thanks to my sister, Dr. Desiree Cox, who helps me to find the wings that I never knew that I had, and to my son David Allens, who gives me the inspiration to fly.

Introduction

Instructional-systems design and project management are different. It is not always easy for the instructional designer to understand how and when to use both disciplines in conjunction. Once the authorization is obtained to design and develop the learning solution, the instructional designer must use the process steps in instructional design with project-management methodology. This book exposes the reader to a comprehensive overview of instructional design using the Instructional-Systems Development (ISD or ADDIE) model and project management techniques based on the framework and standards of the Project Management Institute and the Project Management Body of Knowledge (PMBOK) Guide best practices. Throughout the book, ADDIE and project management are united in a "four step combo." Readers are taught to groove two disciplines to one beat.

Who Should Read This Book

Project Management Skills for Instructional Designers is intended to captivate the interest of the following audience:
- instructional designers,
- training managers and directors,
- training consultants,
- human resources managers,
- performance consultants, and
- project managers.

This practical guide uses the creative approach of storytelling to present the content in a way that is realistic and sequential to the way an instructional designer may work. A case scenario where an instructional designer is given a mandate by the boss to design, develop, and deliver automated sales-management training is the story line around which the two disciplines are applied in the four-step combo.

Step 1 of the Four-Step Combo

Analysis

The first step in The Four-Step Combo introduces the reader to the instructional-systems development model. This introduction includes an overview and a discussion of what to consider when conducting an analysis. The conclusion of a comparative analysis between actual and expected business and performance results is presented in the form of a needs-analysis document. The findings of the needs analysis reveal a gap in knowledge and skill, and the decision is made to design, develop, and deliver a learning solution to close the identified gaps.

Initiating the Project

A review of project initiation is also introduced in the first step of the four-step combo. The presentation format includes the following:

- the definition of project initiation,
- essential ingredients necessary for initiating a project,
- the method that should be used for initiating a project, and
- results of initiating a project.

Sample documents produced as a result of project initiation are presented for review.

Step 2 of the Four-Step Combo

Design

Grooving right along to step two of the four-step combo, where the design document is introduced. This step includes a description of how the design document typically incorporates information from the needs analysis. A sample of a design document populated with information is presented.

Planning

A review of project planning is also presented in the second step of the four-step combo. The presentation format includes the following

- a definition of the project plan and subsidiary plans,

- essential ingredients necessary to develop the project plan and subsidiary documents,

- methods that should be used for developing the project plan and subsidiary documents, and

- results of the project plan and subsidiary documents.

Sample subsidiary documents are populated with information and presented for review.

Step 3 of the Four-Step Combo

Development and Implementation

The design document progresses to development in the third step of the four-step combo. Information on the communication process is presented. This includes describing barriers to effective communication, creating positive expectations, projecting credibility, creating a climate, previewing the content and fitting the message together. Material on validating the course material is also presented.

Executing, Monitoring, and Controlling

A review of project executing, monitoring, and controlling is presented in the third step of the four-step combo. The presentation format includes the following:

- the definition of the project executing, monitoring, and controlling subsidiary plans,

- essential ingredients necessary for project execution, monitoring, and controlling the project plan and subsidiary documents,

- methods that should be used for executing, monitoring, and controlling the project plan and subsidiary documents, and

- the results of project executing, monitoring, and controlling the project plan and subsidiary documents.

Step 4 of the Four-Step Combo

Evaluation and Closing

The four-step combo concludes with a review of evaluation (formative and summative) and project closeout.

The final chapter is dedicated to case analysis. This chapter allows readers to apply the knowledge and skills gained along the way in the context of cases for reinforcement. The net effect of this is on-the-job application for immediate success.

How to Read This Book

Project Management Skills for Instructional Designers is written in a way that gives readers the option of skipping from one step in the combo to the next in an eclectic way. Alternatively, readers may opt to progress through the book by reading according to the sequential presentation of the chapters.

This presentation method works well for just-in-time learning when a quick solution to a situation is required or when a quick reference or job aid is required.

Given the increasing focus on the need for enhanced efficiencies and cost-effectiveness, bringing an effective learning solution in on time, in scope and within budget is of increasing importance to organizations and consultants. *Project Management Skills for Instructional Designers* is a practical guide that provides readers with the expertise to do just that.

Chapter 1
The Crisis

After studying this chapter, you should be able to

- define stakeholders.
- list the persons and/or groups—internal and/or external to the organization—that fit the definition of a stakeholder.
- explain the importance of properly identifying stakeholders at the outset of the project.
- list the procedural steps to follow when designing instructional material.
- define the ADDIE model and explain what procedural steps must be completed within each component of the model.
- list and describe the project management knowledge areas.
- explain how the project management knowledge areas align to the project management process group.

As you read this chapter, be sure that you understand the following terms and ideas.

- Sponsor
- Project Team
- Four-Step Combo
- Project-Management Areas

- Project Manager
- Functional Manager
- ADDIE (ISD) Model
- Project-Management-Process Groups

- Customers/Users
- Project-Management-Process Groups
- PMBOK Guide

The boss drags you into the office after returning from the recent sales retreat, slumps into the chair, and declares, "We have a problem!" You immediately stop what you're doing and give your full attention. Here's the story: Senior leaders are flown in from the head office to host the annual sales retreat designed to pump up sales officers for the upcoming fiscal year. Local and regional sales officers are in attendance at this high-profile meeting.

During the meeting, sales officers are asked direct questions about how they use the new automated sales-management system as a tool to track and monitor their progress toward achieving targets. Responses from sales officers indicate that they are unfamiliar with the functionality of the automated sales-management system. What's more, indications are that the sales officers have no intention of using the system any differently in the upcoming year.

The vice president of sales and the chief executive officer are livid after the discovery and decree that the boss must find an immediate resolution for the problem. The decision is made that the training department will design and develop a learning solution for all sales offices. Attendance for all sales officers will be mandatory. Given that the upcoming fiscal year begins in the next two weeks, the learning solution will need to be designed, developed and delivered within this period. As instructional designer, you are assigned to this project, effective immediately.

Your second question to the boss after the "How could you make such a commitment?" question is, "Could this request really be considered a project?" While this might sound like a basic question, lets begin by reviewing the definition of a project. A project is

- temporary,
- undertaken to create a unique product, service or result, and has characteristics that are developed incrementally as the initiative progresses.

Think about the scenario presented above. Answer the questions below to determine if this scenario fits the definition of a project.

STOP TO COMPLETE ACTIVITY	**Temporary**
	Describe in your own words the situation described by the boss that involves the sales officers.

_____

_____

_____

_____

_____

_____

When are you expected to begin working on this initiative?
Beginning Date _____

What is the deadline to complete this initiative ?
Ending Date _____

The initiative may end when
- *your project objectives are met (i.e. when the training course is launched),*
- *when you terminate your efforts because the objectives cannot be met, or*
- *when the need that generated the idea no longer exists.*

| Note | If your plan to start and end the initiative has a definitive beginning date and end date, the first component of the definition of a project is satisfied. |

| STOP TO COMPLETE ACTIVITY | ## Unique Product or Service

Describe in the space below the unique product, service, or result that this initiative is intended to produce. |

_____
_____
_____
_____
_____
_____

| Note | *Think about this question carefully. You may consider that there are many training programs already established that cater to the same audience. What is unique about this course that will differentiate it from the others?* |

ers? Is it the learning content? Are there any unique characteristics that relate to course delivery? Do you believe that there will be unique or different circumstances that you will encounter throughout this initiative? Because of the unique nature of projects, there may be uncertainties about the products, services or results that the project creates.

If your answer is yes, you have satisfied the second component of the definition of a project.

| STOP TO COMPLETE ACTIVITY | ## Characteristics Developed Incrementally

The third and final component of the definition of a project is that the details and relevant information that you are |

required to know is revealed incrementally as the initiative progresses.

Do you believe that at this moment, you know everything that there is to know about what designing and developing the automated sales-management training program will entail?

Yes   ☐   No   ☐

If your answer is no, you have satisfied the third and final component of the definition of a project.

The proposal to design and develop a solution to close a performance gap fits the definition of a project. This would suggest then, that having knowledge and skills in project management would be a plus in ensuring your successful outcome. Now that you know the definition of a project, let's continue with the definition of the ADDIE instructional-systems development model and project management.

Instructional Design

What Must Be Done

Instructional design processes are typically subdivided into a number of procedural steps which are outlined as follows:

1. Conduct a needs analysis.

2. Assess the relevant characteristics of learners.

3. Analyze the characteristics of a setting.

4. Perform job, task, and content analysis.

5. Write statements of performance objectives.

6. Develop the performance measurements.

7. Sequence the performance objectives.

8. Specify the instructional strategies.

9. Design the instructional materials.

10. Evaluate the training.

Multiple tasks are executed within each procedural step outlined above. The procedural steps may be considered as "what must be done" to design and develop a learning solution. While it is very important to know what tasks must be executed within each procedural step, it is equally important to know at what point in the process these tasks must be performed.

When Do We Do It

Instructional design work is organized sequentially from beginning to end. The components of the ADDIE Instructional-Systems Development Model (ISD) are introduced below

- Analyze
- Design
- Develop
- Implement
- Evaluate

Putting it All Together

The illustration below presents each instructional design procedural step and outlines how these steps relate to the respective component.

Figure 1.1

Analysis	Design	Development	Implement	Evaluate
Training needs analysis Learner analysis Setting analysis Task and content analysis	Objectives specification Test development Sequencing Learning strategy selection	Materials preparation Develop manuals Test prototype	Roll-out initiative	Measure learning outcomes throughout course Generate and analyze evaluation reports

Definition of Project Management

What Must Be Done

Successful project management requires knowledge and skill in a number of areas common to general business management. Some of these areas may be familiar to you like quality management, human resources management, communications management, and risk management. You may be less familiar with some of the others, such as procurement management, integration management, scope management, time management, and cost management.

Tasks to be completed on a project are grouped within these respective knowledge areas according to their relationship with each other. This means that all tasks related to risk are grouped under risk management, tasks related to quality are grouped under quality management, and so on.

Multiple tasks are executed within and across the knowledge areas at different times in the project. In a sense, the knowledge areas can be considered as "what must be done" in a project. While it is very important to know what tasks must be executed within and across each knowledge area, it is equally important to know at what point in the project these tasks must be performed.

When Do We Do It

Project work is organized sequentially from beginning to end, and is grouped within what is described as process groups. These process groups are outlined as follows:

1. Initiating
2. Planning
3. Executing
4. Monitoring and Controlling, and
5. Closing

These process groups are interrelated and dependent on each other. Each project should be guided along a path that follows the same sequence as the process groups.

The Difference Between Projects and Operations

Projects are defined as temporary endeavors with a beginning and an end. Once you have completed all of the steps in designing, developing, and delivering the training program for the launch, your project work would be considered over, and operations would have begun.

Operations are defined as permanent endeavors that produce repetitive outputs. Resources assigned to operations are expected to perform basically the same set of tasks according to the policies, procedures and guidelines that you put in place for your business. For example, if there are set procedures in place for managing the training department, these tasks are completed as assigned according to the operational procedure established for the department. Activities that relate to operations are intended to produce the same product or provide the same repetitive service.

As performance gaps are identified or there is a need to expand the curriculum in the training department, it may become necessary to innovate processes or procedures or develop or upgrade a new product. In this instance, it will be necessary to use project management knowledge and skill to successfully complete this initiative. Once completed, the project is closed out and handed over to the operations aspect of the department.

It is common practice to use projects as a means of executing strategic objectives. These strategic objectives may come about as a result of market demand, technological advance, customer request, regulatory requirements, and/or a business need.

Business and the External Environment

Business affairs are conducted within the context of a larger, and in some instances complex, external environment. This environment may significantly impact the success of projects. Some environmental factors may include but are not limited to

- government or industry standards
- infrastructure
- marketplace conditions
- existing labor force, and
- stakeholders

Stakeholder Influence

Before the project to design and develop a training program kicks off, it is very important to recognize the influence of stakeholders. Stakeholders are defined as people (or organizations) with a "stake" or a vested interest in the project. These are people who are actively involved in the project work or have something to gain or lose as a result of the project. Neglecting to properly identify stakeholders at the outset of the project may mean sudden death for the project and who knows what for you.

STOP TO COMPLETE ACTIVITY
Take a moment now to compile a list of all stakeholders in the automated sales-management training project. Use the list of questions below to assist you with compiling the list.

Are These People Stakeholders?	Yes	No
Learners		
Suppliers		
Employees/Vendors		
The boss		
Your friends		
The project-team members		
The wider local/international community		
Governmental agencies		
Colleagues in other organizations		
Your family		
Employees in other departments in the organization		
The source of the financial funding		

It is important to not only identify the respective stakeholders but also create a plan to manage the influence of the various stakeholders in relation to the project requirements.

Use the space provided below to write the names of the stakeholders on the automated sales management project and rate the level of responsibility and authority that they may have on the success of this initiative.

STOP TO
COMPLETE
ACTIVITY

Name of Stakeholder	Level of Responsibility and Authority on the Project		
	High	Med.	Low

Ready, Set, Off You Go

"So, that's it, you're ready to go," the boss says, rising from the chair, indicating the intention to leave. "The scenario presented fits the definition of a project, the stakeholders are identified, and you understand that we need the training course designed, developed, and delivered to the sales officers in the next two weeks. When will you have the class list on my desk?"

"Just one minute," you say in your most respectful but stern voice. "There's a lot more that must be done before we get to the point of design, development, and delivery."

"Really? Send me an e-mail outlining how you plan to proceed based on what needs to be done."

Just like that, the boss whisks back into the world of the busy executive, leaving you alone to spin straw into gold.

The good news is that you've done this kind of work before, so you immediately get cracking. It occurs to you that the key to success is to effectively put two similar, yet different, disciplines together in one four-step combo. From this idea, ADDIE and project management are united and the "four-step combo" is born.

The Four-Step Combo

The remainder of this book applies the instructional design and project management theory based on the standards of the Project Management Institute in a practical, realistic way that is sequential to the normal way an instructional designer may work. The two disciplines (instructional-systems design and project management) are combined in the four-step combo in a way that is fluid and interconnected.

As the story of the instructional designer and the boss continues, it will be determined if the training course for the sales officers is designed, developed and delivered within the two-week deadline, or better yet, whether there is a justifiable need for a training course in the first place. Grooving to the beat of the four-step combo will result in successful outcomes not only from a theoretical standpoint but also through practical application. Experiences outlined in the following pages may be applied immediately in the work environment.

The Four-Step Combo

	Step 1	Step 2	Step 3	Step 4
Instructional Design	**A** Analysis 1. Training Needs Analysis 2. Learner Analysis 3. Setting Analysis 4. Task and Content Analysis	**D** Design 1. Objectives specification 2. Test Design 3. Sequencing 4. Learning Strategy Selection	**D I** Development and Implementation 1. Materials Preparation 2. Develop Manuals 3. Test Prototype 4. Roll Out Initiative	**E** Evaluation 1. Measure Learning Outcomes Throughout Course 2. Generate and Analyze Evaluation Reports
Project Management	**Initiating** 1. Project Charter 2. Identify Stakeholders	**Planning** 1. Develop Project-Management Plan 2. Collect Requirements, Scope Definition, Create WBS 3. Activity Definition, Activity Sequencing, Activity-Resource Estimating, Activity-Duration Estimating, Schedule Development 4. Cost Estimating, Cost Budgeting 5. Quality Planning 6. Human Resources Planning 7. Communications Planning 8. Risk-Management Planning, Risk Identification, Qualitative Risk Analysis, Quantative Risk Analysis, Risk-Response Planning 9. Plan Procurements	**Executing and Monitoring and Controlling** 1. Direct and Manage Project Execution 2. Monitor and Control Project Work, Integrated Change Control 3. Scope Verification, Scope Control 4. Schedule Control 5. Cost Control 6. Perform Quality Assurance, Perform Quality Control 7. Acquire Project Team, Develop Project Team, Manage Project Team 8. Information Distribution, Performance Reporting, Manage Stakeholders	**Closing** 1. Close Project 2. Close Procurements

Before moving on to the next chapter, take time to complete the discussion questions to understand how the information presented in this chapter may be applied to the next project.

STOP TO COMPLETE ACTIVITY	**Applying to the Next Project**
	Discussion Questions

1. What is the definition of a stakeholder?

2. Who are the persons or groups internal or external to the organization that fit the definition of a stakeholder?

3. Why is it important to properly identify stakeholders and compile an accurate stakeholder list at the outset of the project?

4. What are the procedural steps to follow when designing instructional material?

5. What is the definition of the ADDIE model? What procedural steps must be completed within each component of the model? Explain.

6. How might you define the project management knowledge areas?

7. How do the project management knowledge areas align to the project-management-process groups? Explain.

8. Why should the ADDIE model, the project management knowledge areas and the process groups be used as a four-step combo rather than as discrete models?

9. What are similarities and difference between the ADDIE model and the project-management-process groups?

Activity

The following is an activity that may be completed individually or as a small group activity to assess your comprehension:

1. Review previous projects where accurate stakeholder lists were not compiled and discuss the outcome in those instances.

THE FOUR-STEP COMBO

Step 1

Chapter 2
Analysis

After studying this chapter, you should be able to

- explain why it is necessary to conduct an analysis as the first step in determining performance gaps on the business and individual levels.

- list some questions that may be considered when conducting an analysis.

- describe the first step in assessing the gap on the business level and explain what data should be obtained as a result of using this step.

- describe the second step in assessing the gap on the individual performance level and explain what data should be obtained as a result of using this step.

- list and describe what you should and should not do when it comes to survey administration.

- outline the things that are recommended to be done prior to survey administration.

- state the level and the associated measurement category in the Phillips ROI Evaluation Model.

As you read this chapter, be sure that you understand the following terms and ideas.

- Analysis
- Survey Do's and Don'ts
- Phillips ROI Evaluation

- Compare Expected to Actual Results
- Training-Needs-Analysis Report

You're left with the impression that the boss really believes that a training program for sales officers can be designed, developed, and delivered in two weeks while adhering to the requirements of instructional design and project management. You really have to wonder what they serve at those executive retreats—extra helpings of ridiculous pie topped off with unrealistic expectations?

Never mind that; who knows what commitments the boss made while under duress? Bosses are sometimes reluctant to go back to their senior managers bellyaching about how they can't live up to previous commitments. That leaves you looking at long hours at work. A long, productive hour at work is one thing; wasting time with false starts and rework is not an option. The first thing you need working on your side is a plan—a plan that includes the use of the four-step combo. Step one of the combo covers the areas of needs analysis and initiating the project.

Overview

The instructional-systems development model is introduced in this chapter with an overview and a discussion of what to consider when conducting an analysis. The conclusion of a comparative analysis between actual and expected business and performance results is presented in the form of a needs-analysis document. The findings of the needs analysis reveal a gap in knowledge and skill and the decision is made to design, develop, and deliver a learning solution to close the identified gaps.

Analysis

In the case of the sales officers and the use of the automated sales-management system, analysis is the step used to determine the gap between the profits that should be generated in sales versus the profits that are being generated in sales. Analysis investigates the sales officers' daily work and determines the tasks that they are performing versus the tasks that they should be performing as it relates to the use of the automated sales-management system. Finally, analysis determines the extent to which lack of knowledge and skill is the root cause of the sales officers' performance gaps with the automated sales-management system. Appropriate solutions are recommended accordingly.

Questions to Consider When Conducting an Analysis

Conducting an analysis is an investigation that begins by asking the following types of questions relating to the sales officers and the use of the automated sales-management system:

- How much money is the organization making right now in sales through the use of the automated sales-management system?
- What is the gap between the amount of money that the organization expected to make in sales and the amount of money actually made through the use of the automated sales-management system?
- What tasks are sales officers presently performing while using the automated sales-management system?
- What is the link between sales results and the use or lack of use of the automated sales-management system?
- How many sales officers are presently using the automated sales-management system and how many are not?
- Why aren't sales officers using the automated sales-management system as it is intended?

Step 1 – Compare Expected to Actual Sales Results

The first step in assessing the gap on the business level is to review the expected sales figures and compare these figures to the actual sales figures over the same time period. Data from the sales activity report reveal the following.

Sales Activity Report

Sales Activities	This Period			year to date			
	Annual goal in numbers	# Achieved based on annual	% Achieved based on annual	Annual goal in numbers	# Achieved based on annual	Annual Goal in dollar value	% Achieved based on annual
Calls from Prospect List	500	50	1%	500	50	50,000	.1%
Appointments From Prospect Calls	400	40	1%	400	40	40,000	.1%

Appointments Resulting in Sales	320	20	6%	320	20	32,000	.1%

Step 2 – Compare Expected to Actual Use of the Automated System

After the gap is determined on the business level, the next step is to identify what is happening with the use of the automated sales-management system that might cause the sales figures to look the way they do. How deep and how wide is the gap in the sales officers' performance? What is the root cause or root causes of these gaps? Begin by looking at what sales officers should be doing as outlined in the duty schedule below.

Sales Officers' Duties Relating to the Use of the Automated System

Excerpts from Sales Officers' Duty Schedule
At the end of every day, the automated sales-management system randomly generates a customer call list of prospects obtained from the company's database. The automated sales-management system randomly assigns a list of fifty prospects to each sales officer. The sales officer is expected to do the following on a daily basis with regards to the above:

1. Select the call program link, select the date for the next day, and generate the customer prospect list assigned to the respective officer.

2. Select thirty prospects from the list of fifty prospects.

3. Select the customer preview link.

4. Review the customer preview, including demographic information, products, if the customer is assigned to a specific sales officer, last contact information, and information links.

5. Select customer facts link, review additional customer information and alternate addresses, and relationships.

6. Select customer contact history link and review contact history within the last sixty days.

7. Select customer message link to review and/or record notes specific to a customer.

8. Call the customer and use the call scripts provided under the call scripts tab.

9. Make the appointment and record appointment details in the customer message link.

10. Generate the sale and record the sale in the sales tab.

Data of Actual Use of the Automated System

Excerpts from Reports from the Automated Sales-Management System
The duty schedule reveals what sales officers should be doing. Now to find out what they are actually doing. A good place to start is to once again review the reports from the automated sales-management system. The respective sections of the automated sales management summary report reveal the following information:

Name of Section	Information Captured	#
Prospects Received	Number of prospects assigned to sales officers by the automated sales-management system	50
Actioned	Number of prospects assigned that are actioned inclusive of expired leads	0
In Progress	Number of prospects assigned that have an activity in progress inclusive of pending sales of an offered product	2
Successful Sales	Number of prospects assigned that have resulted in a successful sale of the offered product	20
Unsuccessful Sales	Number of prospects assigned that are recorded with a result "customer not interested" or "canceled"	0

Based on the results of the analysis conducted so far, the boss's initial diagnosis of the problem may be correct. Perhaps the sales officers really do not know how to use the new automated sales-management system, given the data captured from the system. How do you know if this is a case of the sales officers knowing how to use the system and merely refusing to use it? Just because the system isn't being used does not necessarily mean that the officers don't know how to use it: it may mean that they refuse to use it. Further investigation is needed before an accurate conclusion and recommendation can be determined in this case.

Designing, developing and administering a survey to the total population of twenty sales officers is a useful tool in getting the additional information needed.

Do's and Don'ts of Survey Administration

While administering a survey may appear as a straightforward task, past experience has taught valuable do's and don'ts of survey administration as outlined below.

Survey Do's	Survey Don'ts
Use a small sample size and try to get all survey sheets returned.	Don't ask too many questions.
Leave spaces for respondents to insert comments.	Don't use difficult and/or vague language.
Begin with simple, non-threatening questions.	Avoid questions that are worded in a way that the respondent may fear answering correctly.
Meet with respondents prior to administering the survey and explain to them • the purpose. • how the data will be used. • how long the survey will take to complete. • how respondents will benefit. • deadline for returning survey.	Don't ask respondents to put their name or any information that may be used to identify them on the survey sheet.
Make sure instructions are clear.	Don't make the survey too difficult for respondents to complete.
Administer the survey in person to a small group and collect all surveys before respondents leave if possible.	

Actions Completed Prior to Administering the Survey

The following are activities that the instructional designer completed prior to administering the survey that correspond with the recommended survey tips for success.

Conducted Learner Analysis	Met with the department manager and supervisor to learn about the characteristics of the group of sales officers in question. The following information was obtained on behalf of each sales officer: • Job experiences • Aptitude • Motivation • Learning style • Personal qualities and roles in the workplace • Age • Geographic location • Previous knowledge, skill and training exposure • Overall impression of the automated sales-management system
Facilitated Meeting with Sales Officers to Explain the Following	• Purpose of the survey • How survey results will be used • Length of time to complete the survey • Benefit of completing the survey

The total complement of sales officers in the organization is twenty officers. Eighteen of the twenty sales officers were present at the meeting. Outlined below is the survey form that was administered.

Sales Officer Assessment Survey

We want to understand the work environment and the challenges faced by sales officers to help improve job performance and the organization's performance.

Kindly answer the following questions as openly and objectively as possible This survey should take you about ten minutes to complete.

Indicate your job category.

_____

Indicate your job level.
a. Clerical
b. Supervisory
c. Management

1. What is your primary form of sales prospecting?
☐ Telephone

☐ Walk-in/face-to-face

☐ E-mail

☐ Other

2. Do you know about the automated sales-management system?
☐ Yes

☐ No

3. How do you currently acquire knowledge and skill in the use of the automated sales-management system?
☐ Self-study

☐ Job aid

☐ Classroom

☐ Web-based

☐ Informally on the job

Other_____

4. Do you presently use the automated sales-management system to generate prospects from the customer call list?

☐ Yes

☐ No

5. How often do you enter the sales-management system, select the call program link, select the next day's date, and bring up the customer prospect list assigned to you?

☐ At the end of every day

☐ At the end of every other day

☐ Once per week

☐ Once every other week

Other _____

6. How many prospects do you select each day from the list of fifty assigned to you?

_____

7. Do you review the customer profile link including demographic information, products, if the customer is assigned to a specific sales officer, last contact information, and information links before calling the prospect?

☐ Yes

☐ No

8. How do you locate the customer profile link in the automated sales-management system?

_____

_____

9. What link do you use to review additional customer information and alternate addresses and relationships?

_____

10. Why should you use the automated sales-management system?

_____

_____

11. Which are the most important screens to use to capture the results that are tracked and displayed in the automated sales-management system?

_____

_____

12. Do you use the call scripts in the automated sales-management system when calling the customer to make the appointment?

☐ Yes

☐ No

Please comment on your answer.

_____

13. Do you receive recognition from your manager/supervisor when you achieve your sales targets?

☐ Yes

☐ No

Please comment on your answer.

_____

14. Do you receive criticism from your manager/supervisor when you *do not* achieve your sales targets?

☐ Yes

☐ No

Please comment on your answer.

_____

15. Do you lack any tools or resources to achieve your sales targets?

☐ Yes

☐ No

If your answer is yes, what resources do you lack?

_____

16. What obstacles prevent you from using the automated sales-management system as a tool to assist you in meeting your sales targets?

☐ Manpower

☐ Technology

☐ Training

☐ Skills

Other _____

Suggestions/Comments/Concerns

_____

_____

Results from the Survey

The results of the survey are in and are outlined below.

Summary

- Eighteen sales officers of the total population of twenty sales officers completed the survey.
- Two sales officers were away from the office on extended leave.
- 100% survey response rate.

Highlights

- Seventeen sales officers indicated that their primary form of prospecting is walk-in and/or face-to-face.
- While eighteen sales officers indicated that they know about the automated sales-management system, only one sales officer indicated that he used the system.
- The one sales officer who uses the system indicated that he does so once per week and that he has used twenty prospects from the call program list.
- The one sales officer who uses the system indicated that he does review the customer preview link; however, he was unable to describe the steps to locate the customer preview link on the system.
- Eighteen respondents indicated that they do not use the call scripts in the automated sales-management system when calling the customer to make the appointment.
- Eighteen respondents indicated that they do not receive recognition from their supervisor when they achieve their sales targets. The same eighteen respondents also indicated that their supervisor does criticize them when they *do not* achieve their sales targets.

- Eighteen respondents indicated that they do not lack tools or resources. They all indicated that the things that are holding them back from using the automated sales-management system are training and skills.

Conclusion of Needs Analysis

It appears that the boss's initial diagnosis is correct. Lack of knowledge and skill appear to be the root cause of the performance gap. The findings are summarized, presented in the form of a training-needs-analysis report, and sent to the boss via e-mail, as was requested. A sample of the report is presented.

Training-Needs-Analysis Report

Training Requested

- Automated sales-management-systems training for sales officers.

Duties to be Performed

- Identify areas of the home page (e.g. static tool bar, menu bar, etc.).
- Define screens, menus, and buttons.
- Select the call program link, select the next day's date, and generate the customer prospect list assigned to the respective officer.
- Select prospects from the list of prospects.
- Select the customer preview link.
- Review the customer preview including demographic information, products, if the customer is assigned to a specific sales officer, last contact information and information links.
- Select customer facts link, review additional customer information, and alternate addresses, and relationships.
- Select customer contact history link and review contact history within the last sixty days.
- Select customer message link to review and/or record notes specific to a customer.

- Use the call scripts when calling the customer to make the appointment.
- Make the appointment and record appointment details in the customer message link.
- Generate the sale and record the sale in the sales tab.

Expected Performance

Sales Activities	This Period
	Annual Goal in Numbers
Calls from Prospect List	500
Appointments From Prospect Calls	400
Appointments Resulting in Sales	320

Data Collection Method

- Survey
- Sales Records
- Interview

Actual Performance

Sales Activities	This Period	
	# Achieved Based on Annual	% Achieved Based on Annual
Calls from Prospect List	50	1%
Appointments From Prospect Calls	40	1%
Appointments Resulting in Sales	20	6%

Cause of Performance Gap

- Knowledge and Skills

Cost of Training

- $25,000

Benefit of Training

- 320 appointments resulting in sales at an average of $2,000 per sale equals $640,000

Training Proposal

- Classroom instruction

Management Support Recommendations

- Feedback
- Measurement

Narrative

- The chief executive officer and vice president of sales directed the training department to assist in finding and addressing the root cause of performance gaps in sales officers as it relates to the use of the automated sales-management system. A needs analysis was conducted by the training department using data obtained from the sales activity report, sales officer's duty schedule, the automated sales management summary report, interview with managers and supervisors in the sales department, and a sales officers' assessment survey.

- Results from the research confirmed that the sales officers lack knowledge and skill in the use of the automated sales-management system.

- A one-day course in the functionality of the automated sales-management system is recommended. This course will be designed and developed by the in-house instructional designer. The vendor will be commissioned for the use of their subject matter expertise as well as to deliver the training Attendance for all sales officers would be mandatory.

- Close supervision of sales officers supported by one-on-one, group coaching, and positive reinforcement from department supervisors is recommended.

- The course will be evaluated using the Phillips ROI Evaluation model on the following levels:

  Level 1 Reaction and Planned Action

  Level 2 Learning

  Level 3 Application and Implementation

  Level 4 Business Impact

Concluding Needs Analysis

The needs analysis is considered a feasibility study. Senior executives are asked to review this proposal and consider the alternatives presented in the document as a possible solution to the current state.

In the case of the automated sales-management system project, the needs analysis report is prepared by the instructional designer for onward transmittal to the senior executives for approval. Once approved, the next step is to prepare a project charter that, once signed off as approved, acknowledges the grant of organization's resources and authorizes the project to begin.

STOP TO COMPLETE ACTIVITY

Applying to the Next Project

Discussion Questions

1. Why it is necessary to conduct an analysis as the first step in determining performance gaps on the business and individual levels?

2. What are some questions that may be considered when conducting an analysis?

3. What are the steps in assessing the gap on the business level? What data should be obtained as a result of using this step?

4. What are the steps in assessing the gap on the individual performance level? What data should be obtained as a result of using this step?

5. What are some things that you should and should not do when it comes to survey administration?

6. What are some things that are recommended to be done prior to survey administration?

7. What are the levels and the associated measurement categories in the Phillips ROI Evaluation Model?

Activities

The following are some questions/activities that may be completed individually or as a small group activity to assess your comprehension. These concepts are discussed in the context of the case of the sales officers and the automated sales-management system.

1. How comprehensive is the combination of methods and measures used in this needs analysis study? Explain.

2. How appropriate was the needs analysis approach? To what degree did this needs analysis study address the organization's goals and needs?

3. What non-training factors could have an impact on productivity in the workplace? Explain.

4. How credible is the needs analysis process? Critique the data collection methods in this case. How effective were these methods in establishing a need for training?

5. Is there evidence that a thorough job, task, and content analysis was performed? Explain.

Chapter 3
Initiating the Project

After studying this chapter, you should be able to

- state the purpose of the project initiating process and describe the tasks that are performed in this process group.

- list and describe the steps to be completed when identifying stakeholders.

- explain the purpose of the project charter.

- explain who signs off on the project charter and explain the importance of obtaining this sign-off.

- list and describe the information that is included in the relevant sections of the project charter document.

- explain why it is necessary to address all components of the initiating process before deciding which processes are necessary to be completed based on the nature and scope of the project.

As you read this chapter, be sure that you understand the following terms and ideas.

- Initiating Process
- Project Charter
- Identifying stakeholders

Within minutes of sending the e-mail, who should appear? You guessed it, the boss. This time, sporting the biggest grin ever, a far cry from the panic-stricken state you recall in the last appearance. "How's it going?" Is the familiar greeting

"It's going; did you get my e-mail with the training-needs-analysis report attached?" you ask.

"Yeah, I got it-that's why I'm here; you really did a great job on it. Very thorough, detailed, obviously a lot of work went into it. Great job!"

"Thanks," you reply cautiously. You know the boss doesn't usually come into the office just to shoot the breeze; his presence typically translates into more work for you. "So, what's the next step?" you ask.

"You know time is of the essence: the beginning of the fiscal year is just days away. We're still shooting for a two-week turnaround for you to have this material designed, developed, and delivered," the boss replies hastily. "The needs analysis findings support our initial suspicion, With this document in hand, we can see that proceeding to design, develop, and deliver training content is the next step. In addition, based on the research that you've done, the probability of this project succeeding is high."

You get the hint as the boss pauses and looks at you directly. You initiate the next step.

"Well. Then, I'll begin working on the project charter," you reply, appearing to be more enthusiastic than you really are.

"Yes, of course, the project charter is the written acknowledgment that the project exists; we need this document to name you as project manager and to authorize assigning resources to this project," the boss responds.

"I will discuss this training-needs-analysis report with the vice president and the chief executive officer this afternoon after our meeting and get their sign-off at the same time. I will give them my commitment to have the project charter on their desk by the end of the business day tomorrow. I'm off to my meeting, and we'll chat later."

With that, the boss whisks off, faster than a speeding bullet into corporate superhero world.

Overview

It is important to have a goal in mind before planning a project. The goal of the project and product, the persons who will participate in the project, and the scope of the project among other things is crystallized and presented in the project initiation phase. Two project-management processes are included in the initiation process group. These processes include developing the project charter and identifying the stakeholders. Both processes should be considered and performed as a part of project initiation.

In this chapter, project initiation is defined. In addition, the essential ingredients necessary for initiating a project, the method used, and the results obtained from project initiation are also discussed.

Definition of Project Initiation

Just as the name implies, the project initiating process occurs at the beginning of the project, and at the beginning of each project phase for large projects. Project initiation formally recognizes that a project or the next phase of an existing project should begin and that resources should be committed to the project. Project initiation documents include the project charter sign-off used to grant approval to commit the organization's resources to working on the project.

The Project Charter

The project charter documents the business need that the project is initiated to address and justifies the project. The project charter includes a description of the product, service, or result of the project.

Note

Creating the Project Charter

The list below outlines the ingredients necessary to create a project charter. It may not be necessary to use them all. Use only the ones that are relevant based on the description provided below and the nature and scope of the project.

Essential Ingredients

- *The Contract*

    There may be instances when the training department is selling services or products to another organization or individual. In this case, the information presented in the contract should be used when writing the project charter.

    Remember, a contract is only necessary to consider as an input to creating the project charter in instances where the training department is performing a project for an external customer. The contract that will be provided to the buyer typically documents the description of the work that the training department will perform, the conditions under which the work will be executed, the time frame, the price, and other details.

- *Project Statement of Work*

  The project statement of work describes the product, service or result that one company will produce for another organization or individual.

  If the training department is approached and asked to produce a product, service, or result for another organization, or individual, the training department may request that the buyer provide the organization with a project statement of work.

  The training department will use the information in the project statement of work to produce a contract for the organization that commissioned the work. A project statement of work is only produced by the buyer in instances where the work is being produced external to the organization.

- *Enterprise Environmental Factors*

  Enterprise environmental factors refer to factors outside of the project that have or may have significant influence on the project's success. Such factors may include but are not limited to governmental or industry standards, human resources or marketplace conditions.

- *Organizational-Process Assets*

  Organizational-process assets refer to the organization's policies, guidelines, procedures, plans, and/or standards for conducting work. Historical information that represents what the organization has learned from previous projects is also included in this description.

- *Business Case or Business Plan*

  The business case or the business plan typically looks at the business and the cost/benefit analysis as a justified need for the project. A business case or a business plan may be created based on the market demand, organizational need, customer request, technological advance, social need, and/or legal requirements.

When and How to Use Essential Ingredients for Project Initiation

Before moving to the method that should be used to create the project charter, it is important to reinforce a very important point. All of the essential ingredients

Note | *described above do not necessarily have to be used at the same time or in every project.*

The key is to recognize that there are essential ingredients that go into creating a charter document and to know what the essential ingredients are. Exercise judgment in deciding which ingredients or combination of ingredients is needed based on the nature and complexity of the project. That said, lets move on to the method.

The Method

- Expert judgment is the only method needed to be used when creating a project charter. Expert judgment is used to describe the individuals or groups such as stakeholders, practitioners, or groups of people with specialized knowledge or skills in a particular area.

The Result

- *Project Charter*

  When the essential ingredients are combined with the recommended method, the result is a project charter document. The project charter documents the business need that the project is initiated to address, justifies the project, and includes a description of the product, service or result of the project.

  The project charter is often written for sign-off by the project sponsor (the person financing the project) and includes input from key stakeholders. The project charter is not complete without sign-off from the project sponsor, senior management in the business, and key stakeholders.

Outlined below is a sample template of a project charter.

Project Charter Template

Project Name:

Project Manager:

Project Sponsor:

Project Owner (Department):

Version Date:

---

1   Description of Work

Purpose

Business Objectives (measurable outcomes of the project, typically dealing with cost, time, quality (i.e., reduce the cost of delivery by 30%, increase revenues from sales by 2%))

Deliverables (list the high-level products/outcomes whose satisfactory delivery mark the outcome of the project)

In Scope (Clear statement of what the project will include)

Out of Scope (Clear statement of what the project will not include)

Project Success (define what must be done in order for this project to be considered a success by its stakeholders)

_____

_____

_____

Project Milestones (proposed start and end date of project phases and other major milestones)

Critical Milestone	Target Date	Accountability (Name)

Major Known Risks (a risk is anything that may cause the project to fail, this includes things that the project team can and cannot control)

Risk	High	Medium	Low

Assumptions (things that are believed to be true, (e.g., resources will be available to adequately staff the project))

_____

_____

_____

_____

_____

Constraints (things that may limit the project team's options with respect to resources, personnel, schedule and the like)

_____

_____

_____

_____

_____

_____

_____

External Dependencies (will the project's success depend on coordination of efforts with the project team and other individuals or groups)

_____

_____

_____

_____

_____

Summary Budget (estimate the cost and the number of hours required to complete the project work)

_____

_____

_____

_____

_____

Types of Vendor Assistance

_____

_____

_____

_____

_____

_____

2   Roles and Responsibilities

Role	Participant Names	Responsibilities	Forecast Time Investment (in days)

3   Sign-off

Approvals

Role	Signature	Date

STOP TO
COMPLETE
ACTIVITY

Instructions

The following are some questions/activities that you may complete to assess your comprehension of the information and concepts covered so far.

1. Use the information presented so far to populate the project charter template.

2. What information is needed to complete the project charter template in addition to what you presently have?

3. How do you plan to get access to the additional information needed to complete the project charter template?

Benefits of Creating a Project Charter

Although it may appear to be a lot of work, it is highly recommended that project charters are created as a form of documenting the project initiation process for the following reasons:

- The project charter will be used as an input to create the project plan.

- Information presented in the project charter is further elaborated in the project plan. In other words, the project charter document serves as a primary guide for creating the project plan.

- The project charter details what will be done, and the project plan is the document that outlines how it will be done.

- The project charter outlines what is in and out of scope for the project. For example, if you are designing and developing a training program with an e-learning component, and your project charter clearly states that programming and staging the e-learning module is out of scope; this means that these services will not be provided by your company at this time.

- Key information in the project charter serves as a guide when creating the project plan and helps to provide some structure to ensure that the resources are concentrated on what is in scope for the project.

- The project plan is mapped to the project charter to ensure that the critical milestones that were agreed to and signed off in the charter document are achieved within budget. The persons identified as responsible for certain roles are aware of their responsibilities, and the estimated time that they should expect to invest to complete their responsibilities.

- The charter document should be detailed enough to give the sponsor (the person financing the initiative) a clear understanding of what he or she is authorizing.

- Input from stakeholders is included when creating the project charter given that stakeholders have something to gain or lose by the success or failure of the initiative.

That said, let's discuss the last area that should be covered as a part of project initiation. This area is stakeholder identification.

Identifying Stakeholders

Stakeholders may be defined as anyone with a vested interest or who is impacted by the project. It is very important that all stakeholders are identified early in the project and that their levels of interest, expectation, and influence are determined.

> | Note |
> |------|
>
> *The same applies as in the case of creating the project charter. The list below outlines all of the ingredients necessary to identify stakeholders. It may not be necessary to use them all; use only the ones that are relevant based on the description provided below and the nature and scope of the project.*

Essential Ingredients

- *Project Charter*

    This is the document that was previously discussed. The project charter documents the business need that the project is initiated to address and justifies the project.

- *Procurement Documents*

    Procurement documents are considered an essential ingredient for identifying stakeholders when procurement activity is involved in the project. In this instance, stakeholders may include suppliers, vendors, and other parties involved in the contract.

- *Enterprise Environmental Factors*

    Enterprise environmental factors refer to factors outside of the project that have, or may potentially have significant influence on the project's success. Such factors may include but are not limited to organizational culture or customs, governmental or industry standards, human resources or marketplace conditions.

- *Organizational-Process Assets*

    The organization's policies, guidelines, procedures, plans, and/or standards for conducting work are referred to as organizational-process assets. Historical information that represents what the organization has learned from previous projects is also included in this description.

The Method

Two methods are used in this instance: they are expert judgment and stakeholder analysis. Both are reviewed in detail.

- *Expert Judgment*

  Expert judgment is used to describe the individuals or groups such as stakeholders, practitioners, or groups of people with specialized knowledge or skills in a particular area.

- *Stakeholder Analysis*

  Stakeholder analysis is a method used to determine the stakeholders whose interests should be taken into consideration throughout the project. Such analysis uses qualitative and quantitative information to identify all potential stakeholders, their roles, departments, interests, knowledge levels, expectations, and levels of influence. The potential impact or support that each stakeholder may generate is also determined and the appropriate approach and strategy is created based on the relevant data. Some relevant information may have already been gathered when completing the exercises in the previous chapters, so it may only be necessary to refer to previous notes.

The Result

The result of identifying stakeholders is the production of a stakeholder register and a stakeholder-management strategy.

- *Stakeholder Register*

  STOP TO COMPLETE ACTIVITY

  The stakeholder register is a document intended to capture all details related to the identified stakeholders including their identification information, assessment information, and stakeholder classification. This does not have to be an elaborate document. Details may be captured in a document similar to the table presented below.

Stakeholder Name	Contact Information	Level of Influence			Reason
		Hi	Med.	Low	

- *Stakeholder-Management Strategy*

   The stakeholder-management strategy presents the approach that will be used to increase support and minimize negative impacts of stakeholders in the project.

Concluding Project Initiation

With the project charter complete and handed over to the boss, you both have jobs to do. The boss's job is to obtain sign-off on the project charter from all key stakeholders. Your job is to begin working on step two of the four-step combo in anticipation of the boss's reappearance. Step two of the four-step combo includes the design document and project plan.

Applying to the Next Project

Discussion Questions

1. What is the purpose of the project initiating process and what are the tasks that are performed in this process group?

2. What is the purpose of the project charter?

3. What are the essential ingredients, the method, and the result of stakeholder identification?

4. Who signs off on the project charter?

5. Why is it important to obtain sign-off on the project charter?

6. What information is included in the relevant sections of the project charter document?

7. Why it is necessary to address all components of the initiating process before deciding which processes are necessary to be completed based on the nature and scope of the project?

Activities

The following are some questions/activities that may be completed individually or as a small group activity to assess your comprehension. These concepts are discussed in the context of the case of the sales officers and the automated sales-management system.

1. Use the information presented so far to populate the project charter template.

2. What information is needed to complete the project charter template in addition to what is presented?

3. What sections of the reading material did you use to access the additional information needed to complete the project charter template?

4. How helpful is the needs analysis data in completing the project charter template? Explain.

THE FOUR-STEP COMBO

Step 2

Chapter 4
Design Document

After studying this chapter, you should be able to

- explain the purpose of the design document.

- outline the format that design documents are typically presented in and explain the information that is presented in each column of the document.

- describe how the needs analysis report and the design document are linked.

- identify where the data obtained from the needs analysis report appears in the design document.

- explain the concept of task differentiation and sequencing and explain the importance of this process.

- list the steps to follow when differentiating and sequencing tasks.

- list and describe the steps to follow in constructing performance measures.

- explain and give examples of the kind of information that should be contained in a learning strategy.

As you read this chapter, be sure that you understand the following terms and ideas.

- Design Document
- Instructional Method
- Learning Objectives
- Key Points Content/Concepts

- Process/Activity
- Learning Strategy
- Level 3 Evaluation (Phillips ROI)
- Construct Performance Measures

- Task/Content Analysis
- Level 4 Evaluation (Phillips ROI)
- Performance Objectives

- Level 2 Evaluation (Phillips ROI)
- Task Differentiation and Sequencing

The next morning, you arrive to work for an early start. Normal routine. Check e-mails, and there it is, flagged red and sitting in your inbox: a message from the boss. You open it and read the following message, sent from the boss's hand-held BlackBerry at 4:15 a.m.

"Hi there,
Great news, key stakeholder sign-off obtained on project charter. Proceed with design document and project plan. Looking at a quick turnaround. Commitment made to have design document and project plan sign-off by key stakeholders by the end of the week. E-mail documents to me for vetting one day prior to submission. Available by e-mail if you need me. Presently in Abisym on business. We'll chat when I get back in office. Great job keeping the tension on this project!"

You check a few more e-mail messages and then begin working on the design document.

Overview

The design document is introduced in this chapter with a physical description of the document. The link between the needs analysis and the design document is presented to include a description of how the document typically incorporates information from the needs analysis.

The Design Document

The design document outlines the framework of the training program. The design document provides a high-level overview of the product content that will be covered and how it will be treated. Design documents allow key stakeholders to validate the program's objectives, architecture, content, and concepts before the instructional designer moves forward with development.

Design documents are typically presented in a table format with three columns as follows.

Column 1 Learning Objectives	Column 2 Key Points Content/ Concept	Column 3 Process and Activity
Learning objectives describe what the learner is expected to achieve when performing the task. Objectives typically include three parts: • the task statement • the conditions under which the task is performed (e.g., location, available resources, equipment used), and • the standards that describe how well the task must be performed (accuracy, quality, quantity).	Product information, concepts, and criteria to be covered in the respective modules are presented in column two.	This column summarizes the types of learning activities that will be completed in the respective modules.

Column three of the design document contains the instructions that will be used to measure learning throughout the training program. These measures include criterion tests and review tests, the details of which are listed as follows:

Name of Test	Description
Criteria Test	• This is an application exercise or test intended to assess whether or not the objective is achieved during training. • The learner's success with the application is the criterion for deciding if learning is achieved. • The criterion selected must be as job-like and realistic as possible and should match the actions and conditions specified in the objectives as closely as possible. • Criterion tests may be performance or nonperformance. Nonperformance criterion tests are designed to test learner's knowledge only • Examples of nonperformance test question types include multiple choice, matching, fill in the blank, or essay questions.
Review Test	• This is an application exercise or test that is administered at the end of each sub-task based on the task analysis. • A review test is a measure to determine the extent to which subtasks are learned. • Like criterion tests, review tests can be performance or nonperformance and should be as job-like and realistic as possible. Nonperformance review tests are only designed to test learner's knowledge • Examples of nonperformance test question types include multiple choice, matching, fill in the blank, or essay questions.
Post-Course Follow-Up	• Post-course activities are described as activities to be performed to ensure that on-the-job performance objectives are achieved. • Success in this area is determined based on the extent that the learner's activities during training mirrors the performance required on the job.

Column three of the design document also includes instructions on how presentation and application methods are distributed throughout the learning program.

It is customary for the instructional designer to use the one-third, two-thirds ratio: one-third presentation methods, two-thirds application and feedback. Examples of the types of presentation and application methods that may be used are outlined below

Instructional Method	Examples
Presentation methods used to deliver content to the learners	• Lecture • Discussion • Demonstration
Application methods used to give the learners an opportunity to practice, apply, and/or respond to the course content	• Practice exercise • Simulation • Peer review • Role play • Case study • Game • Feedback

Link Between Needs Analysis Report and Design Document

The following data is brought forward from the needs analysis report into the design document as it relates to the automated sales-management training:

Needs Analysis Data	Where It Appears in the Design Document
• Section two of the needs analysis report is essentially the job, task and content analysis around which the learning objectives will be constructed. • Section two is a critical section of the needs analysis report, as this section represents the gap in the sales officers' performance that is linked to lack of knowledge and skill. • The training content is linked directly to the performance gap presented in section two. • The training content is determined based on the learning objectives. The training program is designed on the premise that if the sales officers acquire the knowledge and skill outlined in section two, everything else being equal, they will be able to perform their jobs at the level of the business need. • As such, the benefit of the training figure of $640,000 outlined in section eight of the needs analysis report should be realized.	• Learning objectives column • Key points/contents/concepts column
Needs Analysis Data	**Where It Appears in the Design Document**
• Level 2 evaluation measures will be designed into the course as a direct link to the learning objectives. • Level 3 and Level 4 measures capture expected application and implementation as well as business impact. These evaluation methods will be conducted sixty to ninety days after the classroom session ends.	• Process/activity column

| • Section three of the needs analysis report (expected performance) will be compared to section five (actual performance) to determine the success of the course.

• The same data collection methods outlined in section four of the needs analysis report will be used to capture the Level 3 and Level 4 data. | |

Task Differentiation and Sequencing

Before populating the design document, it is important to differentiate and sequence tasks according to the job, task and/or content analysis. This ensures proper flow of the training program. The steps to follow are outlined below.

- Differentiate between primary tasks (the overall task), main tasks (tasks that must be completed to achieve the primary task), and supporting tasks (tasks that must be completed to achieve the main tasks).
- State whether tasks are psychomotor (physical) or intellectual and/or cognitive.
- Write task statements in the same sequence in which the job is performed.
- Edit task statements and correlate with duties on the sales officer's duty schedule.
- Rate task statements on time spent, difficulty, and level of significance.
- Derive a task importance value for each task (task importance value = difficulty x importance + frequency).
- Rank task statements according to their importance value.

Construct Performance Measures

Another important thing to do before populating the design document is construct performance measures. The steps to complete are outlined as follows:

- Generate a list of knowledge, abilities, skills, and behavior based on the task statements and their importance value (Correlate with information on the respective sales officer's duty schedule).

- Identify entry tasks or prerequisite knowledge (tasks that learners are assumed to already be able to perform).

- Rate whether each knowledge, ability, skill, and behavior is "necessary for new sales officers" and is "practical to expect for novices."

- Rate the degree to which each knowledge, skill, and behavior distinguishes the sales officer with an "expert/teaching" level of proficiency from the "novice/working" level of proficiency.

- Determine the amount of time and practice necessary to acquire knowledge and demonstrate skill and behavior at the desired level given the difficulty, significance, and time spent on the task.

Select Learning Strategy

It is very important to create a learning strategy at the design document stage. A learning strategy is a foundational piece that shapes the architecture of the training program.

The learning strategy takes into consideration the various learning styles as well as the principles of adult learning as outlined below.

Learning Styles	<ul><li>Cooperative Learning – In this instance, learners work as a team teaching and solving problems together.</li><li>Active learning provides all learners with a challenging environment and the opportunity to learn by enjoyment.</li></ul>
Adult Learning Principles	<ul><li>Experience – Adults bring considerable experience into the learning environment. As such, adults need to have ample opportunity to speak, participate, and contribute in their learning experience.</li><li>Self-esteem – Adults have a strong need to maintain self-esteem. As such, adults need validation for the contribution that they make.</li><li>Relevance – Adults desire learning programs that focus on real life situations with relevance to their everyday environment.</li></ul>

	• Benefit – Adults need to see learning as a means to an end rather than as an end in itself.
	• Time Orientation – Adults prefer to engage in learning activities where the learning can be applied now rather than in the distant future.
	• Participation – Adults are engaged by learning environments where there is active participation.
	• Self Directed – Adults are accustomed to being self-directed and typically have as an objective the need to have their expectations met.

The learning strategy for the automated sales-management training is presented as follows:

Prior to Course
- Schedule meeting with manager and supervisor to communicate the essential knowledge related to the training class prior to the sales officers attending class.

During Course
- Introduce the objectives. State the tasks to be performed, including all required resources and material.
- Identify the standard of performance required.
- Present an overview of the training content by identifying how the task related to the automated sales-management system fits into the sales officer's duty schedule.
- State the purpose of the lesson and how it relates to other tasks within the sales officer's duty schedule.
- Explain when, where, and how the respective tasks are to be performed.
- Review any prerequisite material required to perform the tasks that relates to the automated sales-management system.
- Define new terms and provide a glossary for sales officers to use as a job aid.
- Explain the benefits of performing the tasks according to the required performance standards.

- Explain the challenges that may occur and the implications of these challenges on performance in instances where tasks are performed incorrectly.

- List all tasks and sub-tasks based on data compiled in task and content analysis.

- Identify the presentation method that will be used to present content that relates to respective tasks and sub-tasks.

- Identify the application method that will be used and determine how sales officers will apply the content in the case of performance and nonperformance exercises and/or activities.

- Ensure that the one-third presentation, two-thirds application and feedback distribution is adhered to throughout the training.

- Identify how sales officer's performance will be assessed (Level 1 assessment at the end of the classroom session, Level 2 test score data at the end of each exercise as a measure of sales officer's knowledge retention and skill development. On-the-job performance checklist is completed at the end of the training program as a Level 3 measure of performance on the job.)

- Determine that a post-course evaluation questionnaire will be sent to the sales officer and their supervisor and/or manager sixty to ninety days after course completion as a Level 3 measure of application and implementation.

- Capture data from respective automated sales-management system reports for the respective period to obtain Level 3 (application and implementation) and Level 4 (business impact) data.

- Identify whether sales officers will practice individually or in a group during the classroom session.

- List the specific application methods that sales officers will use for performance and nonperformance tests during the classroom session.

- Combine hands-on systems application (using training database) with small group and paper based exercises, inclusive of learning checks and final assessment to teach required knowledge components and measure learning in respective areas.

- Identify the total time required as well as the time required to present and apply knowledge and skill as it relates to each subtask.

- Identify who will observe sales officers during performance and nonperformance test administration (facilitator, other sales officers, self-monitoring or a combination).

- State how the performance will be monitored on the job (performance checklist, etc.)

- Determine if sales officers will receive assistance during application exercises or if they will complete these exercises without the assistance of notes, job aids, or support from the facilitator or other peers in the class.

- Determine how feedback will be obtained and responded to (e.g., other sales officers, self-assessment, discussion, etc.)

- List the questions that the facilitator may use to prompt sales officers to recall key points presented in the material.

- Determine how the facilitator will ensure that sales officers participate in reviewing the objectives.

Concluding Design Document

Once the design document is completed, you send it on to the boss for internal review and sign-off prior to onward transmission to the key stakeholders. With the design document complete and e-mailed to the boss for vetting, you begin working on the project plan and subsidiary documents. There is still much to be done, the deadline is fast approaching, and creating a project plan and subsidiary plans is time-consuming.

A sample of one of the pages of the design document that you submitted to the boss is presented for review.

Sample Design Document, Automated Sales-Management System Training

Content: Session Opener, Introduce Facilitator, Overall Workshop Objectives and Agenda – Big View, Icebreaker, Expectations

Target Audience: Sales Officers

Objectives	Key Points/Content/Concepts	Process/Activity
Training Objective Teach learners to accurately navigate the respective screens of the automated sales-management system to achieve performance targets for appointments and corresponding sales generated from prospect calls. **Session Objectives** Define screens, menus, and buttons and demonstrate knowledge and skill in the functionality of the automated sales-management system at a working level. **Icebreaker** Identify and state specific things that may create barriers to learning and full engagement in the training session. **Expectations** Create, write and explain expectations to be accomplished by the end of the learning program.	**Included in Facilitator Guide** **Introduction** • Welcome the group to the automated sales-management system training session. • Introduce facilitator and co-facilitator for the session. • Inquire about the group's readiness and well-being for the day's session. • State the training objective. *(Write objective on flipchart.)* **Purpose of the Training** Teach learners to accurately navigate the respective screens of the automated sales-management system to achieve performance targets for appointments and corresponding sales generated from prospect calls. **Objective for the Day's Session** Define screens, menus, and buttons and demonstrate knowledge and skill in the functionality of the automated sales-management system at a working level. Hand out session agenda for the day.	**Timing:** • Session opener: 10 Minutes Method – Presentation • Introduce facilitator: 5 Minutes Method – Presentation • Overall workshop objectives and agenda (big view): 5 Minutes Method – Presentation • Icebreaker: 15 Minutes Method – Large Group Activity • Expectations and ground rules: 15 Minutes Method – Large Group Activity • Housekeeping: 5 Minutes Method – Presentation **Facilitator Guide Includes:** Overall workshop objectives and agenda (big view), icebreaker, expectations, ground rules, and housekeeping.

STOP TO COMPLETE ACTIVITY	**Applying to the Next Project**

Discussion Questions

1. What is the purpose of the design document?

2. What is the typical layout of the design document?

3. What type of information is presented in each column of the design document?

4. How are the needs analysis report and the design document linked?

5. Where is the data obtained from in the needs analysis report that appears in the respective columns in the design document?

6. What is the definition of task differentiation and sequencing?

7. Why is task differentiation and sequencing important in designing training programs?

8. What are the steps to follow when differentiating and sequencing tasks?

9. What are the steps to follow when constructing performance measures?

10. What are some examples of the kind of information that should be included in a learning strategy?

Activity

The following is an activity that may be completed individually or as a small group activity to assess your comprehension:

1. Use the template of the design document as a model to create a design document based on a current project in your organization.

Chapter 5
Project-Management Plan

After studying this chapter, you should be able to

- explain the purpose of the project-plan document.
- list the subsidiary documents that are included in the project plan.
- describe the purpose of each subsidiary document that is included as a part of the project-management plan.
- explain why it is necessary to have subsidiary documents included as a part of the project plan.
- explain why it is necessary to address all components of the planning process before deciding which processes are necessary to be completed based on the nature and scope of the project.
- explain why it is necessary to revisit one or more planning processes throughout the life of the project.

As you read this chapter, be sure that you understand the following terms and ideas.

- Scope Plan
- Collect Requirements
- Scope Definition

- Create WBS
- Activities Definition
- Activities Sequencing

- Activity-Resource Estimating
- Activity-Duration Estimating
- Schedule Development

- Cost Estimating
- Determine Budget
- Quality Planning

- Develop HR Plan
- Plan Communications
- Risk-Management Plan
- Risk Identification
- Qualitative Risk Analysis
- Quantitative Risk Analysis
- Risk Response Plan
- Plan Procurement

High-octane java in hand, bags under the eyes, and another day at the office. The long hours needed to move the project along at warp speed are taking their toll. You open your office door and there they are: a huge arrangement of the most beautiful flowers, ah, and the smell of fresh flowers. Who could have sent them?

You put down the java and wish you could just as easily put down the bags under the eyes—but that may require professional treatment and lots of time, neither of which you can access at the moment. Who could have sent these flowers, you wonder? You open the card and the message reads as follows:

"I can only imagine the sacrifice in time and effort that you are making to meet these incredibly tight and demanding deadlines. I cannot tell you how much I appreciate the effort. I hope that these flowers brighten your day and give you the energy that you need to carry on. Arrange to take some time off when this project is done." Signed the boss.

Wow, that was the nicest thing that the boss has done in recent months. With the positive energy emitting from the flowers as the motivator, you begin working on the project-plan document.

Overview

After the goal of the project and other details are documented, and the project charter is signed, the project initiation process is complete and the project to design and develop automated sales-management training is officially in motion.

Collecting specific information about cost, time, quality, risk, and resources to complete the project are issues among others to consider in project planning. Project planning is critical to a successful outcome. Proper planning takes time. Many people do not realize that approximately forty percent of the time allocated to complete your project should be spent in planning. The steps to take when planning a project are introduced in this chapter.

All steps in the respective processes should be considered, although not necessarily performed, as a part of project planning. The decision on the processes to be performed is based on the size and complexity of the project.

The processes necessary to be completed as a part of project planning include developing the project-management plan, collecting requirements, defining scope, creating the work-breakdown structure, defining activities, sequencing activities, estimating activity resources, estimating durations, developing schedules, estimating costs, determining budget, quality planning, developing a human resources plan, communications planning, risk-management planning, identifying risks, performing qualitative risk analysis, performing quantitative risk analysis, planning risk responses, and planning procurements.

The format for this chapter begins with a definition of the project plan and each subsidiary plan. The essential ingredients necessary to develop the respective subsidiary plan and the methods that should be used when developing the respective subsidiary plans are also discussed. Finally, the result of the respective subsidiary plan documents is presented.

Definition of the Project-Plan Document

The project plan describes the overall approach used to plan and manage a project. The planning document gathers information from many sources. All work that is involved in the project is defined, documented, and managed through the project plan inclusive of all subsidiary plans. Each subsidiary management plan contains information that specifically relates to the respective knowledge area. For example, the cost-management plan describes how changes to cost estimates will be reflected in the project budget and how changes or variances with a significant impact should be communicated to the project sponsor or stakeholders.

Relevant stakeholders should be included in the project-planning process given that the stakeholders have skills and knowledge that may be leveraged in developing the project-management plan and any subsidiary plan. It is important that the project team creates an environment where stakeholders can contribute appropriately.

Subsidiary plans may be detailed or simply a synopsis depending on the needs of the project. This chapter details the components of each subsidiary plan with instructions on the essential ingredients that should go into the respective plan, the method that should be used to properly construct the plan, and the corresponding desired result.

Project-Management Plan

The project-management plan is made up of many subsidiary plans that detail how specific areas of the project are to be addressed. The project-management plan is the document that pulls all of the other subsidiary project plans together. All of the processes that are intended to be used during the project are documented in the project-management plan. Outlined are instructions for developing a project-management plan.

Essential Ingredients

The essential ingredients that go into creating the project plan are
- Project charter
- Outputs from many of the processes that the project team intends to use on the project
- Environmental factors outside the organization that may potentially influence the project's success
- Organizational policies, guidelines, procedures, plans and/or standards for conducting work

The Method

- Use expert judgment

The Result

- The project-management plan

Sample Template of a Project-Management Plan

Project Name:		
Prepared by:		
Date		
Version	Date	Comments

1. Summary

- Project purpose and justification
- Objectives
- Overview
- Assumptions and constraints (Link to project-scope statement subsidiary document)

2. Project Plan-Documents Summary

Subsidiary planning documents may only be updated after appropriate review and approval.

Project-scope statement   (Link to scope statement subsidiary document)

Project schedule-management plan   (Link to schedule management subsidiary document)

Project quality-management plan   (Link to quality management subsidiary document)

Project communications-management plan   (Link to communications management subsidiary document)

3. Project Plan Approval/Signatures

Name	Role	Signature	Date

Signatures on this document indicate an understanding of the purpose and content by those signing it. Signatures indicate agreement to use the project-plan document as the formal document.

Collect Requirements

Projects involve completion of many requirements from a variety of sources. Successful completion of these requirements is necessary to meet product and project needs. It is important that information relating to all project and product requirements are recorded and analyzed to fully understand the needs and expectations of the sponsor, customers, and other stakeholders. Information regarding project requirements may be found in the project charter and the stakeholder register. Such information forms the basis of the work-breakdown structure, cost, schedule, and quality planning activities.

Essential Ingredients

The essential ingredients that go into collecting requirements are
- Project charter
- Stakeholder register that lists all of the information that may be used to identify stakeholders who may provide information on detailed project, and product requirements.

The Method

Any of the following items listed below may be used as a method of obtaining information to create the requirements document, requirements management plan, and/or requirements traceability matrix (which are the results of collecting requirements).
- Interviews
- Focus groups
- Facilitated workshop sessions
- Group activity techniques such as brainstorming
- Group decision making techniques
- Questionnaires and surveys
- Observations

- Prototyping – a method of obtaining feedback on requirements by providing a working model of the expected product before it is actually built.

The Result

- *Requirements Documentation*

  Requirements documentation describes the connection between individual requirements and the business need for the project. Components of requirements documentation may include but are not limited to business need for the project or product, functional and non-functional requirements, quality requirements, acceptable criteria, as well as impacts in other entities and other organizational areas.

- *Requirements Management Plan*

  Requirements management plan describes how requirements will be analyzed, documented and managed throughout the project. Information presented in this plan may include detail on how requirements will be planned, tracked, and reported and how configuration management activities will be conducted.

- *Requirements Traceability Matrix*

  The requirements traceability matrix is a table that links each requirement to their business and project objectives ensuring that each requirement adds business value. This method allows requirements to be tracked by their origin and traced throughout the project life cycle. This ensures that the requirements approved in the requirements documentation are delivered at the end of the project.

Scope Definition

Defining the scope is capturing in words a description of all of the work that will be involved in the project. It is very important to be as specific as possible about the work and only the work that will be produced during and as a result of the project. The purpose of defining the scope is to produce a scope statement that details the project's objectives, deliverables, and requirements.

Essential Ingredients

The essential ingredients that go into defining the scope are

- Project charter

- Requirements documentation that describes the connection between individual requirements and the business need for the project.

- Organizational policies, guidelines, procedures, plans, and/or standards for conducting work.

The Method

- Any of the following listed below may be used as a method of obtaining information to create the scope statement and update the respective project documents:

  - *Product Analysis*

    Product analysis is used to convert the product description and objectives into requirements and deliverables.

  - *Alternatives Identification*

    Alternatives identification is a technique used to discover alternative ways or methods of achieving the project's objectives.

  - *Expert Judgment*

    Expert Judgment is used to describe the individuals or groups such as stakeholders, practitioners, or groups of people with specialized knowledge or skills in a particular area.

  - *Facilitated Workshops*

    Facilitated sessions are structured meetings that may bring together key functional stakeholders. During these meetings, the facilitator guides the participants through a series of pre-defined steps to arrive at a result that is created, understood, and accepted by all participants. These meetings present a good opportunity for relationship building and for establishing trust among participants.

The Result

- *Project-Scope Statement*

  The project-scope statement is the document that details the project's objectives, deliverables, and requirements. The project-scope statement is designed to give everyone concerned with the project a clear impression of what the outcome of the project is intended to produce.

- *Project Documents Update*

  The project documents that may be updated include but are not limited to stakeholder register, requirements documentation, and requirements traceability matrix.

Sample of a scope statement template

Project-Scope Statement

Project Name:	
Prepared by:	
Date	

1. Project Purpose (brief overview of the purpose and justification of the project)

2. Product Description

3. Business Objectives

4. Project Description (provide sufficient detail to properly refine the project)

Includes: (Deliverables breakdown is presented below)

Does Not Include:

Project Completion Criteria: (Describes what will be completed in terms of deliverables and their characteristics or what constitutes as successful completion. This may be listed by phase.)

External Dependencies: (One project or deliverable may be dependent on another project or deliverable, or information from one or several sources. This linkage must be identified and its progress monitored.)

Assumptions: (Examples of assumptions may be but are not limited to support and attention will be provided by the sponsor, resources will be available to adequately staff the project, etc.)

Constraints: (All projects have constraints that must be identified at the outset. Describe limits in terms of people, money, time, material, quality, and the like.)

5. Project Milestones (define project milestones and target dates)

Project Milestones	Target Date

6. Project Approach (describe the structure of the project (e.g., phased approach and provide a brief description of the method that will be used). For example, will there be outsourcing of jobs, hiring temporary resources, etc.)

Primary Plans: (Describe whether the project will have formal plans—for example, project schedule, budget, quality plan, risk plan, etc.)

Scheduled Meetings: (Will there be scheduled meetings to be held during the project? Include a description of the meetings and how often they are to be held)

Scheduled Status Reports: (Will there be status reports produced and distributed during the project? Include a description of these reports, the purpose, and how often they will be produced.)

Issues Management: (Include general information about how issues will be managed in this project. How will issues be tracked, prioritized, assigned, resolved and communicated to the relevant persons? Will there be an Issues Log to describe the issue, the owner, resolution and status of the issue?)

Change Management: (Include general information on how requests for change in the project will be managed (e.g., Will a Change Request Log be established by the project manager to track all changes associated with the project effort? Will all change requests be reviewed to determine possible alternatives and costs? Who will approve changes?))

Communication Management: (Include a general statement on how communication will be managed in the project. Will the project manager present the project status report to the project sponsors on a weekly basis? Will there be ad hoc meetings when issues or change issues arise? How will the project sponsor be notified of urgent issues?)

Procurement Management: (Include a general statement on how goods and services needed for the project will be obtained; this includes how many items, when and by what means will each good or service be obtained. What types of contracts, if any, will be used? How will cost estimates be determined? Which procurement documents will be used?)

Resource Management: (Include a general statement of how resources will be managed: list all goods and services required in the project along with cost estimates and quality information. Which goods and services will be obtained from sources outside of the organization? Who will be assigned to the project and when?)

The purpose of this document is to provide a vehicle for documenting the initial planning efforts for the project. It is used to reach a satisfactory level of mutual agreement among the project manager, the project sponsor, and the project team with respect to the objectives and scope of the project before significant resources are committed and expense incurred.

Authorizations (signatures indicate an understanding of the purpose and content of this document by those signing it and agree to this as the formal project-scope statement document)			
Name	**Role**	**Signature**	**Date**

Version History		
Version	**Date**	**Comments**

Instructions

STOP TO COMPLETE ACTIVITY

Think about a project that you are presently working on. Use the information from your business plan or business case as well as from the project charter and complete the project-scope statement template.

Take your time and be thorough in completing this document. We will rely heavily on the scope statement to produce other project planning documents.

Create Work-Breakdown Structure (WBS)

Now that you have produced the scope statement that clearly defines the work that the project will and will not do, the next step is to use the scope statement to create the work-breakdown structure document.

The work-breakdown structure is a comprehensive review of the project scope. This document subdivides the major project deliverables and project work into smaller, more manageable components called work packages. Work packages are the lowest level of the work-breakdown structure. As a general rule, the lowest level tasks should have durations between two and twenty-two days and an effort that that does not take one person more than one week to complete.

Essential Ingredients

The essential ingredients that go into creating the work-breakdown structure are

- Project-scope statement

- Organizational policies, guidelines, procedures, plans and/or standards for conducting work.

- Requirements documentation that describe the connection between individual requirements, and the business need for the project.

The Method

- Decomposition is the only suggested method to be used in creating the work-breakdown structure. Decomposition is a technique that involves breaking down the deliverables into smaller, more manageable components of work.

  Breaking down the work results in more accurate estimates that relate to time, cost, and resources needed to complete project work. Decomposition may also result in accurate controls and performance measures.

The Result

- *Work-Breakdown Structure*

  The work-breakdown structure (WBS) is described as a deliverable orientated, hierarchical decomposition of the work to be executed by the project team. The work-breakdown structure is used to create the required deliverables in accordance with the project's objectives.

- *Work-Breakdown Structure Dictionary*

  The work-breakdown structure (WBS) dictionary is created as a support and can be viewed as the companion document to the work-breakdown structure (WBS). The work-breakdown structure (WBS) dictionary should include the code of accounts identifier, description of the work attached to each component, organization (or individual) responsible for completing each component of work, and list of schedule milestones.

- *Scope Baseline*

  The scope baseline for the project is the approved project-scope statement, the work-breakdown structure, and the work-breakdown structure dictionary.

- *Updates to the Project Documents*

  The project documents that may be updated include but are not limited to requirements documentation that may need to be updated if approved change requests result from the creating the WBS.

Example of an Excerpt from a Work-Breakdown Structure

1. Develop Learner Guide and Facilitator Guide

   1.1 Develop and insert tests for learner and facilitator guide

   1.2 Use content presentation strategy to develop learner and facilitator guide

   1.3 Internal review, approval, and sign-off of learner and facilitator guide

2. Training

   2.1 Create system documentation

   2.2 Create training materials

   2.3 Train users

Instructions

1. Review the information that you have captured in category four of your scope statement under the heading project completion criteria. This information describes what will be completed in terms of deliverables and their characteristics or what constitutes successful completion.

2. Look at the example of the work-breakdown structure presented above.

3. Use the information in your scope statement and subdivide the major project deliverables and project work into smaller, more manageable components called work packages.

4. Work packages are the lowest level of the work-breakdown structure. As a general rule, the lowest level tasks should have durations between two and twenty-two days and an effort that that does not take one person more than one week to complete.

5. Make sure that your work-breakdown structure is complete. Review the following list to assess the completeness of your work-breakdown structure:

   ▪ one owner may be assigned to each of the lowest tasks

   ▪ outputs are evident for each task and are clearly defined

   ▪ the project is broken down at the level that can be tracked

   ▪ quality may be monitored through performance criteria associated with each output

   Include tasks for the following:

   • approval cycles

   • key project meeting

   • management and/or customer interfaces

   • quality inspections

   • project reviews and closing

The process of creating the work-breakdown structure is an excellent team-building activity as many discussions should take place to ensure that all parties are aware of what needs to be done to produce the required deliverables.

The work-breakdown structure document will continue to be updated during the planning and schedule development process. This generally happens as the project progresses and additional information that must be incorporated into the work-breakdown structure is known.

Work-Breakdown Structure for Your Training Initiative

Activity Definition

Once the scope is defined and the work is broken down into work packages, the next step is to break down the work packages into smaller components. This process is referred to as activity definition.

Activity definition relates to the specific actions that must be performed to produce the project deliverables. Activity definition provides the basis for estimating, scheduling, executing, and monitoring and controlling the project work.

Essential Ingredients

The essential ingredients that go into the process of activity definition are

- Organizational policies, guidelines, procedures, plans and/or standards for conducting work

- Environmental factors outside the organization that may potentially influence the project's success

- Scope baseline for the project is the approved scope statement, the work-breakdown structure, and the work-breakdown structure dictionary

The Method

There are several suggested methods that may be used to produce the activity lists, the activity attributes, and the milestone lists (outcomes of the activity definition process). The methods are as follows:

- *Expert Judgment*

  Expert judgment is used to describe the individuals or groups such as stakeholders, practitioners, or groups of people with specialized knowledge or skills in a particular area.

- *Decomposition*

  Decomposition is a technique that involves breaking down the deliverables into smaller, more manageable components of work.

- *Templates*

  Many organizations and industries have work-breakdown templates that they use for their respective projects. Using a work-breakdown structure from a previous project may be an option.

- *Rolling Wave Planning*

   Rolling wave planning involves planning work that must be performed in the near future in greater detail than the work that must be performed in the distant future.

The Result

- *Activity Lists*

   Activity lists outline all scheduled activities to be performed for the project. This gives the project team the information that they need to know about the exact tasks to be performed.

- *Activity Attributes*

   Activity attributes are an extension of the activity lists. Activity attributes describe the characteristics of the activities such as the activity identifier, code, and/or assumptions or constraints associated with the respective activity. Conditions linked to predecessor activities (activities that come before the activity in question) and successor activities (activities that come after the activity in question) are also described. Information about resource requirements and the person responsible for completing the respective task is described as activity attributes.

- *Milestone Lists*

   Milestones are described as major accomplishments in the project and signal the completion of a major deliverable or some other key event in the project. Approval sign-off is typically considered as a milestone.

Excerpt of a Work-Breakdown Structure with Activity List – Automated Sales-Management Training

1.1 Develop Learner Guide and Facilitator Guide

   1.1.1   Develop and Insert Tests, Learner Guide, and Facilitator Guide

      1.1.1.1 Write learning check tests in learner guide.

      1.1.1.2 Write learning check correct responses in facilitator guide.

      1.1.1.3 Write key concepts list for learner guide.

      1.1.1.4 Write case study questions for learner guide.

1.1.1.5 Write case study responses for facilitator guide.

1.1.1.6 Link every test question to learning and performance objectives, learning content, and data from task and content analysis.

1.1.1.7 Write test items according to precise and measurable standards.

1.1.1.8 Determine the number of questions needed for each primary objective to ensure that the learner really knows the material.

Instructions

1. Review the information that you have captured in completing your work-breakdown structure to the work-package level. This information describes what will be completed in terms of deliverables and their characteristics or what constitutes successful completion.

2. Look at the example of the work-breakdown structure including activity lists presented above.

3. Use the information in the work packages of your work-breakdown structure to decompose to the level of creating activity lists.

4. Make sure that your activity lists are complete.

Work-Breakdown Structure and Activity Lists for Your Training Initiative

_____

_____

_____

_____

_____

_____

_____

_____

_____

_____

_____

_____

_____

_____
_____
_____
_____
_____
_____
_____
_____
_____
_____
_____
_____
_____
_____
_____
_____
_____
_____
_____
_____
_____
_____

Activity Sequencing

Once the activities are defined, the related dependencies are identified, sequenced, and documented. Dependencies are the relationships between tasks that affect the overall timing of a project. You cannot determine the duration of a project by summing up the duration of all of the tasks (or activities) because some tasks in a project happen simultaneously while others happen sequentially. For example, it is recommended that you complete a task and content analysis before you create a design document. However, you can develop the learner guide and arrange logistics for the launch of the training program at the same time in the project. It is important to anticipate and establish relationships called dependencies among tasks in a project that relates to your training initiative. After you have defined the tasks or activities, the next step is to sequence them and determine the dependencies.

Essential Ingredients

The essential ingredients that go into sequencing activities are the following:

- *Project-Scope Statement*

  The project-scope statement is the document that details the project's objectives, deliverables, and requirements.

- *Activity Lists*

  An activity list outlines all the scheduled activities to be performed for the project within the scope-of-work description of each activity and identification code or number.

- *Activity Attributes*

  Activity attributes are an extension of the activity lists. Activity attributes describe the characteristics of the activities.

- *Milestone Lists*

  Milestones are described as major accomplishments in the project, and signal the completion of a major deliverable or some other key event in the project.

- *Organizational-Process Assets*

  The organization's policies, guidelines, procedures, plans, and/or standards for conducting work are referred to as organizational-process assets.

The Method

There are several methods that may be used to produce a schedule-network diagram and update project documents that are produced as a result of sequencing activities. These methods are presented as follows

- *Precedence Diagramming Method*

  This method is used in critical-path methodology for constructing project schedule networks. Precedence diagrams use boxes or rectangles to represent activities called nodes. The nodes are connected with arrows showing the dependencies between activities. Precedence diagramming is used to determine dependencies or logical relationships as follows:

    Finish-to-start (FS) – This relationship says that the predecessor activity must finish before the successor activity can start. This is the most commonly used dependency in the precedence diagramming method.

Start-to-finish (SF) – This relationship says that the predecessor activity must start before the successor activity can finish.

Finish-to-finish (FF) – This relationship says that the predecessor activity must finish before the successor activity finishes.

Start-to-start (SS) – This relationship says that the predecessor activity must start before the successor activity can start.

- *Schedule-Network Template*

Many organizations and industries have schedule-network templates that they use for their respective projects. Using a schedule-network template from a previous project is also an option.

- *Dependency Determination*

The types of dependencies used to define the sequence among activities are outlined below:

Mandatory dependencies – these are inherent to the nature of the work being done.

Discretionary dependencies – these are usually established based on best practices within a particular industry or aspect of the project where an unusual sequence is desired.

- *Applying Leads and Lags*

Lags delay successor activities and require time to be added either to the start or finish date of the scheduled activity. Leads speed up the successor activity and require time to be taken off of either the start date or the finish date of the scheduled activity.

The Result

- *Project Schedule-Network Diagram*

The result of activity sequencing is the creation of a schedule-network diagram. The project schedule-network diagram is a schematic display of the project's activities and dependencies.

- *Project Document Updates*

The project documents that may be updated include but are not limited to activity lists, activity attributes, and risk register.

Instructions

1. Review the information that you have captured in completing your work-breakdown structure to the work- package level as well as your activity lists.

2. Determine the dependencies between tasks and indicate these dependencies beside the respective tasks.

3. Use the identifier codes beside each activity to avoid having to write the name of the tasks multiple times.

4. It is important to not skip any of the previous steps that we have reviewed together. If you have skipped a few steps in the previous exercises, now is a good time to go back and make sure that your information is thorough and accurate.

Activity-Resource Estimating

STOP TO COMPLETE ACTIVITY

Before proceeding to activity-resource estimating, let's take a moment to recap what is covered so far.

1. You have defined the scope and produced the scope statement. What is the purpose of the scope statement?

_____

_____

_____

_____

2. Next, you broke down the major deliverables into more manageable components. What is the lowest level of a work-breakdown structure called?

_____

_____

_____

_____

3. You continued the process by breaking down the work packages. What is the next step to complete after the work-breakdown structure is complete and what are the results of this step?

    _____

    _____

    _____

    _____

4. Then, you sequenced the activities. What is produced as a result of activity sequencing?

    _____

    _____

    _____

    _____

Your next step is to estimate the resources that will be required to complete the relevant activities. Activity-resource estimating is the area that involves establishing accurate estimates of the types and quantities of resources required to perform each schedule activity. The number of resources that you assign to a task may affect the duration of the task. For example, if one person takes four hours to set up the training room, adding a second person may reduce the time needed to set up the training room by half. Setting up the training room may still require four hours of effort, but two resources can work simultaneously to complete the task in half the time. A resource-driven task is a task whose duration is affected by adding or subtracting resources.

On the other hand, the duration of some tasks is unaffected by the number of people or other resources you devote to them. These tasks have a fixed duration that is determined by the nature of the task, (the time it takes to download the software on you computer for example). That said, let's review the essential ingredients, the method, and the result for estimating resource activity.

Essential Ingredients

*   *External Environment*

    External environmental factors refer to factors outside of the project that have the potential to significantly influence the project's success.

*   *Organizational-Process Assets*

The organization's policies, guidelines, procedures, plans, and/or standards for conducting work are referred to as organizational-process assets.

- *Activity Lists*

  An activity list outlines all the scheduled activities to be performed for the project within the scope-of-work description of each activity and identification code or number.

- *Activity Attributes*

  Activity attributes are an extension of the activity lists. Activity attributes describe the characteristics of the activities such as the activity identifier, code assumptions, or constraints associated with the respective activity.

- *Resource Availability*

  In this instance all resources including human and material resources must be determined. This includes the types of resources, and the quantities. Information on the availability of the resources must be determined in advance.

- *Resource Calendars*

  Resource calendars document information on the resources that are available during a planned activity period. These resources include people, equipment, and material. Resource calendars may include information on resource experience and/or skill level as well as various geographical locations from which the resources originate and when they may be available.

The Method

There are several methods that may be used to produce the results of activity-resource estimating. These methods are presented as follows:

- *Expert Judgment*

  Expert judgment is used to describe the individuals or groups such as stakeholders, practitioners, or groups of people with specialized knowledge or skills in a particular area.

- *Alternatives Analysis*

  Alternatives analysis helps the project team to consider the other alternatives that may be available to realize the desired outcome.

- *Published Estimating Data*

  Estimating data may include industry rates, estimates, organizational guidelines, price agreements, and the like.

- *Project Management Software*

  Project management software may be used to assist with estimating resources needs and documenting resource availability.

- *Bottom-up Estimating*

  Bottom-up estimating is a process of estimating individual schedule activities or costs and then adding these together to come up with a total estimate for the work package. Every schedule activity is estimated individually and then added together to derive a total.

The Result

The result of activity-resource estimating is

- *Activity-Resource Requirements*

  Activity-resources requirement describes the types and quantity of resources required for each scheduled activity.

- *Resource-Breakdown Structure*

  The resource-breakdown structure is a hierarchical structure of the resources required for the project. These resources are identified by category and resource type.

- *Project Document Updates*

  Project documents that may be updated include but are not limited to activity lists, activity attributes, and resource calendars.

 Instructions

1. Use the details that you compiled in the activities that you previously completed to populate the activity-resource requirements template for your training project.

Activity Resource Requirement Template

Task/ Activity #	Task/Activity Description	Type of Resources		Estimated # of Resources
		Human Resources	Equipment	

Activity-Duration Estimating

Once you have identified your resource requirements, which include the types and quantities, the next step is to estimate the duration that these resources are required for. Activity-duration estimating is concerned with estimating the number of work periods that will be needed to complete individual schedule activities.

The Method

There are several methods that may be used to estimate activity duration; they are outlined below.

- *Enterprise Environmental Factors*

  Enterprise environmental factors refer to factors outside of the project that have the potential to significantly influence the project's success.

- *Organizational-Process Assets*

  The organization's policies, guidelines, procedures, plans, and/or standards for conducting work are referred to as organizational-process assets.

- *Project-Scope Statement*

  The project-scope statement is the document that details the project's objectives, deliverables, and requirements.

- *Activity List*

  An activity list outlines all the scheduled activities to be performed for the project within the scope-of-work description of each activity and identification code or number.

- *Activity Attributes*

  Activity attributes are an extension of the activity lists. Activity attributes describe the characteristics of the activities such as the activity identifier, code assumptions or constraints associated with the respective activity.

- *Activity-Resource Requirements*

  Activity-resources requirement describes the types, and quantity of resources required for each scheduled activity.

- *Resource Calendar*

  The resource calendar includes the type, quantity, availability, and capability of equipment, material, and human resources.

The Method

There are several methods that may be used to estimate activity duration:

- *Expert Judgment*

  Expert judgment is used to describe the individuals or groups such as stakeholders, practitioners, or groups of people with specialized knowledge or skills in a particular area.

- *Top-Down Estimating or Analogous Estimating*

  Analogous estimating is also referred to as top-down estimating. This is a form of expert judgment that uses the actual duration of a similar activity completed on a previous project to determine the duration of the current activity. Top-down estimating is a good technique to use early in the project-planning process when many of the details of the project are being fleshed out.

- *Parametric Estimating*

  Parametric estimating is a form of estimating that multiplies the quantity of the work by the rate to determine the activity duration.

- *Three-Point Estimates*

    The three point estimate uses the average of a three point estimate to arrive at the final estimate. The three points are most likely, optimistic, and pessimistic. The most likely estimate assumes that the activity may be completed as planned. The optimistic estimate presents a faster time frame in which the activity may be completed. The pessimistic estimate assumes the worst happens and the activity takes much longer than planned to be completed.

- *Reserve Analysis*

    Reserve analysis refers to the process of adding a portion of time or a set of work periods to the activity to account for schedule risk.

The Result

The following is the result of activity-resource estimating:

- *Activity-Duration Estimates*

    Activity-Duration Estimates are assessments of the likely number of work periods that it will take to complete a scheduled activity.

- *Project Document Updates*

    Project documents that may be updated include but are not limited to activity attributes and assumptions made in developing the activity-duration estimates such as skill levels and availability.

STOP TO COMPLETE ACTIVITY **Instructions**

1. Use the details that you compiled in the previous activity where you estimated the resources that you will need for your project.

2. Populate the additional column of the template below with information on the duration that you anticipate these resources will be needed for.

3. Look at the method described above that you should use to arrive at your estimates.

4. Remember, you are not required to use all of the options listed under the methods section; use only the one(s) that you are familiar with or that apply in the your specific project.

5. The objective is that at the end of the day, you have a pretty accurate idea of the likely number of work periods that it will take to complete the scheduled activity.

Activity Resource Requirement Template Including Duration Estimates

Task/ Activity #	Task/Activity Description	Type of Resources		Estimated # of Resources	Estimated Duration	
		Human Resources	Equipment		Days	Hrs.

Schedule Development

The steps covered so far are intended to establish the foundation necessary to develop the schedule. Schedule development requires analyzing activity sequences, duration, resource requirements, and schedule constraints to create the project schedule.

Essential Ingredients

The following are essential ingredients required to develop the schedule:

- *Enterprise Environmental Factors*

  Enterprise environmental factors refer to factors outside of the project that have the potential to significantly influence the project's success.

- *Organizational-Process Assets*

  The organization's policies, guidelines, procedures, plans, and/or standards for conducting work are referred to as organizational-process assets. Historical information that represents what the organization has learned from previous projects is also included in this description.

- *Project-Scope Statement*

    The project-scope statement is the document that details the project's objectives, deliverables, and requirements.

- *Activity List*

    An activity list outlines all the scheduled activities to be performed for the project within the scope-of-work description of each activity and identification code or number.

- *Activity Attributes*

    Activity attributes are an extension of the activity lists. Activity attributes describe the characteristics of the activities such as the activity identifier, code assumptions or constraints associated with the respective activity.

    - *Project Schedule-Network Diagrams*

        The project network diagram is a schematic display of the project schedule activities, and respective dependencies.

    - *Activity-Resource Requirements*

        Activity-resources requirement describes the types and quantity of resources required for each scheduled activity.

    - *Resource Calendars*

        The resource calendar includes the type, quantity, availability, and capability of equipment, material, and human resources.

    - *Activity-Duration Estimates*

        Activity-duration estimates are assessments of the likely number of work periods that it will take to complete a scheduled activity.

The Method

- *Schedule Network Analysis*

    The project schedule is produced as a result of the schedule network analysis. The schedule network analysis involves calculating early and late start dates and early and late finish dates for project activities.

- *Critical-Path Method*

    Critical-path method is a schedule network analysis technique. This technique is used to determine the amount of float or schedule flexibility for each of the network paths. The calculation of the earliest start date and finish date and latest start and finish dates for each activity is the basis of this calculation.

- *Schedule Compression*

  Schedule compression is a form of mathematical analysis that is used to shorten the project schedule without changing the project scope. This allows the related activities to be accomplished sooner than estimated.

- *What-if Scenario Analysis*

  What-if scenario analysis uses a series of different "what-if" questions to present activity assumptions to determine the project duration.

- *Resource Leveling*

  Resource leveling is a technique that is used when resources are limited or time is constrained and when specific schedule needs must be met. Resource leveling allows the project manager to assign under-allocated resources to multiple tasks to keep them busy and reduce the work of over allocated resources.

- *Critical-Chain Method*

  Critical-chain method is a technique that modifies the project schedule to account for limited resources. This technique typically schedules high risk tasks early in the project so that problems are identified and addressed right away.

  - *Applying Leads and Lags*

    Lags delay successor activities and require time to be added either to the start or finish date of the scheduled activity. Leads speed up the successor activity and require time to be taken off of either the start date or the finish date of the scheduled activity. As the project schedule is created, there may be a need to adjust lags and leads.

  - *Scheduling Tool*

    Automated scheduling tools speed up the scheduling process by generating start to finish dates based on the inputs of activities, network diagrams, resources, and activity durations.

The Critical Path

The critical path is a visual representation (usually drawn in red) used to identify the tasks that must be completed on time for the project to be completed by the project's end date. If any task on the critical path becomes delayed, the end date of the project becomes delayed. Knowing where your critical path tasks are at any point during the project is essential to staying on track.

A simple example can be used to explain the critical path. Suppose you are planning a training session off site. The following are some tasks that may be involved and the time that you may need to complete them

Send out the e-mail and confirm trainee attendance	5 hours
Confirm the logistics and other services at the location	3 hours
Clear the inventory of training material from the shipping company	5 days
Hire the truck to bring the inventory to the location	3 days
Set up the training room with literature and material	30 minutes

The shortest task, set up the training room with literature and material, only takes thirty minutes. Theoretically, you can delay setting up the training room with literature and material until thirty minutes before the start of the training session. For the purpose of this example, delaying this task will not delay the start of the training session as you complete this task at the end of the longest task, which is clearing the inventory of training material from the dock.

The task of setting up the training room with literature and material is not on the critical path; however, you cannot delay clearing the inventory from the shipping company without delaying the start of the training session. Therefore the task of clearing the inventory is on the critical path. In this simple example, only one task appears on the critical path; typically a series of tasks that cannot afford delays form an entire critical path.

Float, also called slack, is the amount of time that you can delay a task before that task moves onto the critical path. In the preceding example, the thirty-minute-long task of setting up the training room with literature and material has slack.

This task can slip for a few hours, even a few days, and the training session will still start on time. However, if you wait until the last half hour of the day of the training session to set up the room, that task will have used up all of its slack and will then move onto the critical path.

Project Schedule

Schedules may be created using project management software or other applications. They may range from complex and intricate to the basic representation.

Instructions

1. Use the details that you compiled in the previous activities to complete the schedule template below.

Project Schedule Template

Task	Responsible	Duration Estimate of Days	Baseline		Actual		# of Days Delay From Baseline	Reason for Delay	Action Steps
			Start	Finish	Start	Finish			

The Result

- *Project Schedule*

  The project schedule determines the start and finish dates for each project activity in addition to the resource assignments. Once the project schedule is signed off and approved, it becomes the baseline for the remainder of the project.

- *Schedule Data*

  The documenting and supporting data for the schedule is referred to as the schedule data. This data includes information on project milestones, schedule activities, activity attributes, and assumptions and constraints regarding the schedule.

- *Schedule Baseline*

  The schedule baseline is the specific version of the project that is accepted and approved by the project team and the stakeholders. The project progress and task completion is monitored and tracked against the baseline, which is the measurement that is used to determine whether the project is on track.

- *Project Document Updates*

  Project documents that may be updated include but are not limited to activity-resource requirements, activity attributes, project calendar and risk register.

Cost Estimating

Once you have completed your schedule, you can now move to estimate your cost. Cost estimating requires developing an approximation of the costs of the resources needed to complete project activities. By now I am sure you can see how important it is to be thorough when completing the previous steps that included creating the scope statement, the work-breakdown structure, defining the activities, sequencing the activities, estimating the resources, and duration, and creating the schedule.

Tasks that are inadvertently omitted in previous steps may not be included in the cost estimating, which may cause you potential challenges in the future. Be sure to be as thorough as possible in completing all steps to minimize challenges in executing the schedule in the future. If at this point you realize that you have made some errors or may have inadvertently omitted some necessary information, review and correct your work before moving on to the next sections. That said, let's review the essential ingredients necessary for cost estimating.

Essential Ingredients

- *Enterprise Environmental Factors*

  Enterprise environmental factors refer to factors outside of the project that have or may significantly influence the project's success.

- *Organizational-Process Assets*

  The organization's policies, guidelines, procedures, plans, and/or standards for conducting work are referred to as organizational-process assets.

  Historical information that represents what the organization has learned from previous projects is also included in this description.

- *Scope Baseline*

  The project-scope statement is the document that details the project's objectives, deliverables, and requirements.

- *Project Schedule*

  The project schedule determines the start and finish dates for each project activity in addition to the resource assignments. Once the project schedule is signed off and approved, it becomes the baseline for the remainder of the project. The type and quantity of resources and the amount of time that those resources will apply to completing the project work are major factors in determining project cost. Activity-duration estimates may also affect time-sensitive cost estimates such as union labor with regularly expiring collective bargaining agreements or materials with seasonal cost variations.

- *Human Resources Plan*

  Project costs are determined in part by the type and quantity of resources, and the amount of time that those resources are needed to complete the project work. Schedule activity provides critical information necessary to assist in determining project costs. Project staffing attributes, hourly rates, and related reward and recognition are necessary components for developing the project cost estimates.

- *Risk Register*

  The risk register is a document that contains a list of identified risks, list of potential responses, root causes of the risks, and updated risk categories. The risk register should be reviewed to consider risk mitigation costs. Risks that may be either threats or opportunities may have an impact on both activity and overall project costs.

The Method

The following methods may be used to estimate costs:

- *Expert Judgment*

    Expert judgment is used to describe the individuals or groups such as stakeholders, practitioners, or groups of people with specialized knowledge or skills in a particular area.

- *Analogous Estimating*

    Analogous estimating is also referred to as top-down estimating. This is a form of expert judgment that uses the actual cost of a similar project completed in the past as a basis for estimating the cost of the current project. Analogous cost estimating is frequently used to estimate cost when there is a limited amount of detailed information available on the project.

- *Bottom-Up Estimating*

    Bottom-up estimating is a technique that estimates costs associated with every activity individually and then rolls them up to derive a total project estimate.

- *Parametric Estimating*

    Parametric estimating is a form of estimating that uses project parameters in a mathematical model to predict total costs. Parametric estimates are calculated by multiplying the quantity of the work by the rate to calculate the cost estimates.

- *Project Management Software*

    Project management software such as cost-estimating software applications, spreadsheets simulation, and statistical tools automate the mathematical calculations necessary to perform cost estimating.

- *Vendor-Bid Analysis*

    Vendor-bid analysis is the process of gathering information from vendors to assist in establishing estimates. This information may be obtained by requesting bids or quotes or by working with trusted vendor sources for estimates.

- *Reserve Analysis*

  Reserve analysis refers to the process of adding a portion of time or a set of work periods to the activity to account for schedule risk.

- *Cost of Quality*

  Cost of quality is a technique used to determine the costs incurred to ensure quality. Cost of quality includes prevention costs, appraisal costs, and the cost of quality planning, and quality control. Cost of rework, lost of reputation, cost of warranty work and waste are also costs of quality. This information is necessary to prepare the schedule activity cost estimate.

- *Three-Point Estimates*

  The accuracy of a single-point activity cost estimate may be improved by estimating uncertainty and risk. The program evaluation and review technique (PERT) uses three estimates (most likely, optimistic, and pessimistic) to define an approximate range for an activities cost. Cost estimates based on a PERT analysis equation or even a simple average of the three points may provide more accuracy as the three points may clarify the range of uncertainty of the cost estimate.

The Result

Cost estimating is intended to produce the following results:

- *Activity-Cost Estimates and Supporting Detail*

  Activity-cost estimates are amounts usually stated in monetary units that reflect the cost of the resources needed to complete the project activities.

  Cost estimating may include the following supporting detail:

  o work estimated

  o how the estimate was developed or the basis of the estimate

  o assumptions made about the estimates or the method used to determine them

  o constraints, and

  o stated estimates within ranges

- *Basis of Estimates*

  It is important to ensure that the level of detail provided and the documentation supporting cost estimates provide a clear and complete understanding of how the cost estimate was derived. Supporting detail may include documentation of the basis of the estimate, all assumptions made, known constraints, range of possible estimates, and an indication of the confidence level of the final estimate.

- *Project Document Updates*

  Project document updates include but are not limited to the risk register.

Instructions

1. Use the details that you compiled in the previous activities where you estimated the resources and the duration that those resources will be needed for to complete your project.

2. Populate the respective sections in the template below with details that reflect the cost of the resources needed to complete the project activities.

Project Resource Plan

Project Name	
Prepared By	
Date	
1. Resource Profiles (provide the general description of the major resources that will be needed to proceed with the project. These resources may include people, equipment, facilities, materials and supplies, and services.)	
People	
Equipment	
Facilities	
Material and Supplies	

Services

2. Project Resource Information (determine cost, availability, estimated quantity, and output of people and equipment for each of the resources needed.)

Resources	Cost Estimate	Availability	Quantity	Output	Known Constraint

3. Resources Staffing Plan (identify the type of people that you need for the project on a monthly basis.)

Type of People	Month	Month	Month	Month	Month	Month	Month	Month

4. Project Resource Plan Signatures

Project Name	
Project Manager	

I have reviewed the information contained in the project resource plan and agree

Name	Role	Signature	Date

The signatures above indicate an understanding of the purpose and content of this document by those signing it. By signing this document, they agree to this as the formal project resources plan document.

Cost Budgeting

You may have presented rough cost estimates in your project charter based on previous research conducted. However, as you elaborate the project in greater detail during the planning process, you may find that the initial cost projection may not be as accurate as it could be. Cost budgeting requires adding up the estimated costs of individual activities or work packages to establish a cost baseline. You may have already discovered that outputs in some project-management processes are used as input into others. This is also the case in cost budgeting.

Essential Ingredients

The following are essential ingredients that go into cost budgeting.

- *Organizational-Process Assets*

  The organization's policies, guidelines, procedures, plans, and/or standards for conducting work are referred to as organizational-process assets. Historical information that represents what the organization has learned from previous projects is also included in this description.

- *Project-Scope Statement*

  The project-scope statement is the document that details the project's objectives, deliverables, and requirements.

- *Activity Cost Estimate and Supporting Detail*

  Activity-cost estimates are amounts usually stated in monetary units that reflect the cost of the resources needed to complete the project activities.

- *Project Schedule*

  The project schedule determines the start and finish dates for each project activity in addition to the resource assignments. Once the project schedule is signed off and approved, it becomes the baseline for the remainder of the project.

- *Resource Calendars*

  Resource calendars address specific individual or groups of resources and determine their availability for the period in question.

- *Contract*

  The contract includes information related to the products and/or services that must be purchased and their associated costs. These costs are used when developing the budget.

- *Basis of Estimates*

  There should always be a basis for cost estimates that should be specified in detail. This specification should capture both indirect and direct costs. Any basic cost assumptions that pertain to what is included and/or excluded in the project should be specified in the basis of estimates.

The Method

The following method is used for cost budgeting:

- *Expert Judgment*

  Expert judgment is used to describe the individuals or groups such as stakeholders, practitioners, or groups of people with specialized knowledge or skills in a particular area.

- *Cost Aggregation*

  Cost aggregation is the process of adding up all of the schedule activity costs estimates at the work-package level (the lowest level of the work-breakdown structure). Costs at the work-package levels are then totaled to the highest work-breakdown structure component level (such as the control accounts).

- *Reserve Analysis*

  Reserve analysis is the process of establishing contingency reserves such as the management contingency reserve that are allowances for unplanned but potentially required changes.

- *Funding-Limit Reconciliation*

  Funding-limit reconciliation is the process of reconciling the amount of funds spent with the amount of funds budgeted for the project.

- *Historical Relationships*

  Parametric and analogous estimates are used in conjunction with project parameters to develop mathematical models that predict total project costs. Analogous and parametric models are most likely to be accurate when historical information used to develop the model is accurate, the parameters used in the model are readily quantifiable, and the models are scalable allowing them to work in project phases as well as on large and small projects.

The Result

The following are produced as a result of completing the cost budgeting process:

- *Cost Baseline*

The cost baseline is a time-phased budget that is used as a basis for measuring, monitoring, and controlling overall cost performance on the project. The cost baseline is developed by adding the costs of the work-breakdown structure according to time periods.

- *Project Funding Requirements*

  Project funding requirements are the total amount of money spent on the project. This amount may be determined as an annual or quarterly amount, and is derived from the cost baseline. Funding requirements may be established to exceed the baseline by a margin to allow for early progress or cost overruns. The total funds required are those included in the cost baseline plus the management contingency reserve amount.

- *Project Document Updates*

  The documents that may be updated include but are not limited to the risk register, cost estimates, and project schedule.

STOP TO COMPLETE ACTIVITY

Instructions

1. Use the details that you compiled in the previous activities to create the cost baseline, which is a time-phased budget that is used as a basis for measuring, monitoring and controlling overall cost performance on the project.

2. Feel free to use any templates that you may already have in place for your organization.

3. If you do not have any templates in place, you may use the templates below to assist you in this exercise.

Project Budget Form

Activity Code	Project Task	Labor Hours	Labor Cost $	Material Cost $	Travel Cost $	Other Cost $	Total Cost Per Task

Project Cumulative Cost Chart

Month of Project	Projected Monthly Cost	Projected Cumulative Cost	Actual Monthly Cost	Actual Cumulative Cost

Quality Planning

Quality planning addresses the management of product and project quality. Product quality measures and techniques are specific to the type of product produced by the project. Failure to meet product and project requirements may result in negative consequences.

Quality planning identifies which quality standards are relevant to the project and determines what system the project will adopt to ensure that the quality standards are satisfied. Quality planning activities should take place in conjunction with performing other project-management processes.

For example, proposed changes in the product to meet quality standards may result in impact to cost, resource, schedule, and other estimates. That said, let's take a look at the essential ingredients that go into quality planning.

Essential Ingredients

- *Enterprise Environmental Factors*

    Enterprise environmental factors refer to factors outside of the project that have or may significantly influence the project's success.

- *Organizational-Process Assets*

    The organization's policies, guidelines, procedures, plans, and/or standards for conducting work are referred to as organizational-process assets.

- *Project-scope baseline*

  The project-scope statement is the document that details the project's objectives, deliverables and requirements.

- *Stakeholder Register*

  Stakeholder register is a list of information that may be used to identify stakeholders who can provide information on detailed project and product requirements.

- *Cost Baseline*

  The cost baseline is a time-phased budget that is used as a basis for measuring, monitoring, and controlling overall cost performance on the project. The cost baseline is developed by adding the costs of the work-breakdown structure according to time periods.

- *Schedule Baseline*

  The project schedule determines the start and finish dates for each project activity in addition to the resource assignments. Once the project schedule is signed off and approved, it becomes the baseline for the remainder of the project.

- *Risk Register*

  The risk register is a document that contains a list of identified risks, list of potential responses, root causes of the risks and updated risk categories. The risk register should be reviewed to consider risk mitigation costs. Risks that may be either threats or opportunities may have an impact on both activity and overall project costs.

The Method

Several methods may be used to complete the quality planning process. They are presented as follows.

- *Cost/Benefit Analysis*

  The cost-benefit trade off is considered in the quality planning process. Preventing defects saves time and money in the short and long run. This is one of the primary benefits of meeting quality requirements. Additional benefits include stakeholder satisfaction, lower costs, high productivity, and less rework.

- *Benchmarking*

Benchmarking is a standard of performance measurement in which similar activities performed in previous projects are compared to the activities in the present project.

- *Design of Experiments*

  Design of experiments is a statistical technique that identifies the variables that will have the greatest impact on overall project outcomes. Design of experiments analyzes several variables at once allowing the project manager to change all or some of the variables at the same time. This technique gives the project manager the opportunity to determine which combination will produce the best results at a reasonable cost.

- *Cost of Quality*

  The cost of quality is described as the total cost to produce the product or service of the project in accordance with the quality standards identified for the project. The cost of quality includes all costs associated with all work necessary to meet the product requirements.

- *Additional Quality Planning Tools*

  Some additional quality planning tools include brainstorming, and the nominal group technique, flowcharts, affinity diagrams, force field analysis, matrix diagram, and prioritization matrices.

- *Control Charts*

  Control charts are used to determine whether or not a process is stable or has predictable performance. Upper and lower specification limits are based on requirements outlined in the contract, and reflect the maximum and minimum values allowed.

  Flowcharts are typically used to track repetitive activities required for producing manufactured lots; however, they may also be used to monitor cost, and schedule variances, volume, and frequency of scope changes.

- *Statistical Sampling*

  In statistical sampling a part of the population that is identified for sampling is selected for inspection. The frequency and size of the sample is typically determined during the quality planning process. This allows the cost of quality to include the number of tests, expected scrap, etc.

- *Flowcharting*

  Flowcharting represents the relationship among process steps in a graphical format. All flowcharts show activities, decision points, and the order of processing.

- *Proprietary Quality Management Methodologies*

  Quality management methodologies include Six Sigma, Lean Sigma, Quality Function Deployment and many other methodologies.

The Result

The result of quality planning is the following:

- *Quality-Management Plan*

  The quality-management plan identifies the quality standards that will be adopted by the project. The quality plan describes how the quality policy will be implemented, and managed. Quality planning is included in the creation of the quality-management plan.

- *Quality Metrics*

  Quality metrics describes what is being measured, and how it will be measured. Failure rates, reliability, availability, test coverage, and defect density measurements are other types of quality metrics that are measurable.

- *Quality Checklists*

  Quality checklists provide a means of determining whether the required steps in the process are followed. Each step is checked off of the list upon completion. Checklists may be industry specific or specific to a particular activity. Organizations often have standard checklists that they may use for certain projects.

- *Process Improvement Plan*

  Process improvement plans focus on finding inefficiencies in a process or activity. Once the inefficiency is found, the goal is to eliminate it. Examples of inefficiencies may be waste, and non-value-added activities

- *Project Document Updates*

  The project documents that may be updated include but are not limited to the stakeholder register and the responsibility assignment matrix.

Instructions

1. Use the details that you compiled in the previous activities to create the quality-management plan for the project.

2. Feel free to use any templates that you may already have in place for your organization.

3. If you do not have any templates in place, you may use the template below to assist you in this exercise.

Project Quality-Management Plan

Project Name:	
Prepared By:	
Date:	

1. Organization's Quality Policy

2. Project Quality Definition (describe how the customer defines quality in this project. How will the customer know quality when they see it? What is more important: schedule, cost, scope, or quality of deliverables?)

3. Deliverables and Acceptable Criteria (list significant deliverables, including contract deliverables and milestone checklist. Describe the acceptance criteria for each deliverable. List quality standards where relevant.)

Deliverables	Acceptance Criteria/Applicable Standards

4. Quality Assurance Activities (define quality assurance activities for the project)

- What steps will you take to ensure that quality is built into the product?
- How will you ensure that the level of testing required is completed for this project?
- Is there a test plan?
- How will you ensure that requirements are correct, complete, and accurately reflect the needs of the customer?
- How will you verify that specifications are accurate and represent the project quality requirements?
- What steps are in place to ensure that the vendor is supplying deliverables at the standards that are required for the project?

5. Project Monitoring and Control
• What audits and reviews are required and when will they be conducted? • How will you report and resolve variance from the project requirement standard? • What will you measure to determine if the project is out of scope? • What will you measure to determine if the project is within budget? • What will you measure to determine if the project is within schedule?

6. Project Quality Plan Signatures			
I have reviewed the information contained in the project quality plan and agree			
Name	**Role**	**Signature**	**Date**

The signatures above indicate an understanding of the purpose and content of this document by those signing it. By signing this document, they agree to this as the formal project quality plan document.

Human Resources Management Plan

As we progress through the planning processes we must consider the human resources aspects. The human resources management plan describes how human resources requirements for the project will be met. This document outlines the processes for organizing and managing the project team. Involving team members early in the process may add expertise during the planning process that often strengthens commitment to the project. The type and number of project members will tend to change depending on the duration of the project.

Essential Ingredients

The following are essential ingredients that go into creating the human resources management plan:

• *Enterprise Environmental Factors*

Enterprise environmental factors refer to factors outside of the project that have or may significantly influence the project's success.

- *Organizational-Process Assets*

  The organization's policies, guidelines, procedures, plans, and/or standards for conducting work are referred to as organizational-process assets.

- *Activity-Resource Requirements*

  Activity-resources requirement describes the types and quantity of resources required for each scheduled activity.

The Method

- *Organization Charts and Position Descriptions*

Organizational charts may be presented in three ways:

    1. Hierarchical

        Hierarchical charts are designed in a top-down format where the organizational or department head is at the top, the management employees who report to the head are next, and the lower level employees are represented on the next level.

    2. Matrix-Based Charts

        Matrix-based charts show the type of resource and the responsibility that the respective resource has on the project. A responsibility assignment matrix (RAM) is used to graphically display the information. A RACI chart is a type of RAM. The letters in the acronym RACI represent the following designations shown on the chart:

        R = Responsible for performing the work

        A = Accountable, the person responsible for producing the deliverable or work package

        C = Consult, someone who has input to the work or decisions

        I = Inform, someone who must be informed of the decision or results

    3. Text-Orientated Formats

        A position description is an example of a text-orientated format. This type of format is useful when there is a considerable amount of detail to record. This type of format outlines the role, responsibility, and authority of the resource.

- *Networking*

  Networking may be described as informal interaction with others in the organization or industry. Networking is an effective technique to use in project management.

- *Organizational Theory*

  Organizational theory describes the various theories that provide information and insight on human behavior as it relates to individual, team, and/organizational dynamics.

The Result

- *The Human Resources Plan*

  The human resources plan identifies and documents the project roles, responsibilities, and reporting relationships from a human resources standpoint. The staffing management plan is also included in this document.

STOP TO COMPLETE ACTIVITY

Instructions

1. Use the details that you compiled in the previous activities to create the human resources plan for the project.

2. Feel free to use any templates that you may already have in place for your organization.

3. If you do not have any templates in place, you may use the template below to assist you in this exercise.

Human Resources Plan

Project Name					
Project Manager					
Stakeholders/Project-Team Members					
Project Tasks/ Activities	Person Name	Person Name	Person Name	Person Name	Person Name
	Role	Role	Role	Role	Role

Communication Planning

Effective communication is essential to the success of a project. Communication planning includes the processes required to ensure timely and appropriate collection, retrieval and dissemination of project information. The process of communication planning is designed to ensure that the relevant stakeholder needs are met. In addition, an effective communication plan includes information on who needs what information, instructions on when they need this information, and who will be responsible for disseminating this information. These factors are important to the project's success.

Essential Ingredients

The following are essential ingredients necessary for creating the communication plan:

- *Enterprise Environmental Factors*

  Enterprise environmental factors refer to factors outside of the project that have or may significantly influence the project's success.

- *Organizational-Process Assets*

  The organization's policies, guidelines, procedures, plans, and/or standards for conducting work are referred to as organizational-process assets.

- *Project Charter*

  The project charter documents the business need that the project is initiated to address and justifies the project. The project charter includes a description of the product, service, or result of the project.

- *Procurement Documents*

  If a project is the result of a procurement activity or based on an established contract, the parties in that contract are the key stakeholders, and as such should be included as a part of the project stakeholders list.

The Method

- *Expert Judgment*

  Expert judgment is used to describe the individuals or groups such as stakeholders, practitioners, or groups of people with specialized knowledge or skills in a particular area.

- *Stakeholder Analysis*

  Stakeholder analysis is a method used to determine the stakeholders whose interests should be taken into consideration throughout the project. Such analysis uses qualitative, and quantitative information to identify all potential stakeholders, their roles, departments, interests, knowledge levels, expectations, and levels of influence. The potential impact or support that each stakeholder may generate is also determined and the appropriate approach and/or strategy is created based on the relevant data.

The Result

- *Stakeholder Register*

  The result of identifying stakeholders is the production of a stakeholder register and a stakeholder-management strategy. The stakeholder register is a document intended to capture all details related to the identified stakeholders including their identification information, assessment information, and stakeholder classification.

- *Stakeholder-Management Strategy*

  The stakeholder-management strategy presents the approach that will be used to increase support and minimize negative impacts of stakeholders in the project. This process involves the key stakeholders at the outset.

 STOP TO COMPLETE ACTIVITY

Instructions

1. Use the details that you compiled in the previous activities to create the communication plan for the project.

2. Feel free to use any templates that you may already have in place for your organization.

3. If you do not have any templates in place, you may use the template below to assist you in this exercise.

Project Communication Plan Template

Some fields include instruction on how to populate the document

Project Name:	
Prepared by:	
Date:	

1. Project Purpose

2. Business Need

3. Communication Principles

Include principles to ensure consistency in messages and tone in your communication.
Communication will be:

- straightforward and honest in keeping with your organization's values and standards for two-way communication,

- consistent to all stakeholder groups and/or audiences,

- written from the perspective and voice of the intended stakeholder and/or audience using a conversational tone,

- promoted as a means to increase acceptance,

- concise, direct, and produced in a manner that is easily understood so as to be mindful of the time constraints of the audience, and

- timely and cost-effective to reflect user preference.

4. Communication Objectives
• Promote and explain the benefits of the initiative.
• Gain support and cooperation for the initiative informing stakeholders how and where they fit into the process.
• Promote two-way discussion and face-to-face communication as a means of increasing acceptance and sustaining change.

5. Target Audience
• General staff.
• Managers and/or supervisors.
• Executive and/or senior management.

6. Key Messages
Key messages should be stand-alone statements that are true and relevant regardless of the audience. They should be supported by facts, easy to understand, free of jargon, easy to remember, concise, direct, and powerful.
Your key message should answer the following questions: • Why is this initiative being done?
• What is the initiative about?
• What are the benefits for customers?
• What is in it for the organization?
• How will the organization be supported in making this change?
• When will this initiative start and when will it be over?
• How will the organization know when it is successful in the initiative?

7. Change Implications

This initiative represents change for the organization and the employees given that it represents something new. In preparing this section, outline the nature of the change in terms of the following:

- How will using the new method(s) differ from what employees are used to doing?

- What practices have to change? (Detail this in list form)

- What behaviors will have to change? (Detail this in list form)

- What expectations will have to change? (Detail this in list form)

- Describe how employees can participate in and even shape the change through communication. Clearly outline the reason for change to help the audience understand why they are being asked to do what they are being asked to do.

8. Challenges and Opportunities

What factors may help or hinder the plans regarding communication? Think in terms of the audience's point of view. What might they have heard in the past? What might their expectations be? Do they trust or are they cynical? Are they positioned to understand what is being communicated? Can they do what is being requested?

Audience	Message (Explain launch, build expectations, enroll in the program, communicate program success, follow-up, etc.)	Channel (face to face, e-mail, flyers, notices remote broadcast etc.)	Responsible	Delivery Date

9. Project Communication Plan Signatures

I have reviewed the information contained in the project quality plan and agree

Name	Role	Signature	Date

The signatures above indicate an understanding of the purpose and content of this document by those signing it. By signing this document, they agree to this as the formal project communication plan document.

Risk-Management Plan

We are nearing the end of the project planning exercise. There are a lot of steps. At the same time, it is important to remember that project planning does require approximately forty percent of the time that is dedicated to completing a project. The more thorough the project plan, the easier it is to execute, monitor and control. Risk-management planning and plan procurements conclude the project-planning process.

Risk-management planning includes the processes necessary to increase the probability and impact of positive events and decrease the probability and impact of negative events in the project.

Essential Ingredients

There are several essential ingredients that go into the risk-management planning process. These ingredients are outlined below for your review. Many if not all of these essential ingredients are covered previously in the preceding processes.

- *Enterprise Environmental Factors*

  Enterprise environmental factors refer to factors outside of the project that have or may significantly influence the project's success.

- *Organizational-Process Assets*

  The organization's policies, guidelines, procedures, plans, and/or standards for conducting work are referred to as organizational-process assets.   Historical information that represents what the organization has learned from previous projects is also included in this description.

- *Project-Scope Statement*

  The project-scope statement is the document that details the project's objectives, deliverables, and requirements.

- *Cost-Management Plan*

  The cost-management plan describes how costs are managed. Cost estimating and cost budgeting are included in the creation of the cost-management plan.

- *Schedule-Management Plan*

  Project-time management is concerned with all processes required to ensure that the project is completed on time. This aspect of the project is managed within the context of the schedule-management plan.   Activity definition, activity sequencing, activity-resource estimating, activity-duration estimating, and schedule development are included in the creation of the schedule-management plan.

- *Communications-Management Plan*

  The communications-management plan describes the communications needs of the stakeholders, including timing, frequency, and methods of communication. Communications planning is the process for determining the information and the communications needs of the project stakeholders. This plan identifies who needs what information, when they should get the information they need and who should be responsible for giving this information to them. It is important to identify the information needs of the stakeholders, and determine a suitable means of meeting those needs.

The Method

There is only one method that may be used to complete the risk-management planning process. This method is outlined below.

- *Planning Meetings and Analysis*

    These meetings take place with the project team, stakeholders, functional managers, and others who may have involvement in the risk-management planning process. The plans for performing risk-management activities are discussed and determined in these meetings and are documented for the risk-management plan.

Typical issues discussed and agreed to in these meetings are

- risk-cost elements are developed for inclusion in the project budget.

- schedule activities associated with risk are developed for inclusion in the project schedule.

- risk responsibilities are assigned.

- templates for risk categories are defined or modified for the respective project.

- definitions of terms (probability, impact, risk types, risk levels, and so on) are developed and documented.

- the probability and impact matrix is defined or modified for this project.

The Result

The result of the risk-management planning process is the production of the risk-management plan.

- *Risk-Management Plan*

    Careful risk planning is essential to the success of any project. Risk-management planning is the process of deciding how to approach, and conduct risk-management activities. This is necessary to ensure that the appropriate amount of time and resources is dedicated to the necessary risk-management activities. Risk-management planning is particularly necessary to establish an agreed-upon basis for evaluating risks. The risk-management plan includes risk identification, qualitative risk analysis, quantitative risk analysis, and risk-response planning.

Instructions

1. Use the details that you compiled in the previous activities to create the risk-management plan for the project.

2. Feel free to use any templates that you may already have in place for your organization.

3. If you do not have any templates in place, you may use the template below to assist you in this exercise.

4. There may be some fields in this template that you may not be able to complete at this time. You will be redirected to populate these fields as you progress through the other areas of risk that relate to project planning.

Project Risk-Management Plan Template

Some fields include instruction on how to populate the document

Project Name:	
Prepared by:	
Date:	
1. Risk Identification (identify risks through discussion with all major stakeholders)	
2. Risk Categorization (group the risks into categories that the project manager and the project team may create)	
3. Risk Probability and Impact Assessment (Enter all risks into the risk response plan document. Assess the risk event for each risk identified in terms of likelihood of occurrence (risk probability) and its effect on project objectives if the risk occurs.)	

4. Risk Prioritization (risks that meet the threshold criteria should be noted in the risk register.)

5. Risk-Response Planning (identify a plan for each risk in the risk register that is above the risk threshold.)

Determine the options and actions to reduce the likelihood or consequences of impact to the project's objectives

Determine the response based on a cost/benefit analysis

Describe the actions to be taken to mitigate the risk

Describe the signs and symptoms that may be indicators of a risk event occurrence

Describe the actions to be taken when the risk event occurs (contingency plan)

Assign responsibility for each agreed-upon response

Assign a due date where risk responses are time sensitive

Determine the impact on project budget and schedule and make appropriate changes or additions to the project plan

Incorporate this information into the risk register

6. Risk Management Strategy
Document the dates and the actions taken to mitigate the risk
Document the actions taken when the risk event occurred (contingency plan)
Document any subsequent actions taken
Incorporate this information into the risk register

7. Risk Monitoring (establish systematic reviews and schedule them in the project schedule, ensuring the following reviews:)
Ensure that all requirements of the risk-management plan are being implemented
Assess currently defined risks as defined in the risk register
Evaluate effectiveness of actions taken
Validate previous risk assessment (likelihood and impact)
Validate previous assumptions
State new assumptions
Identify new risks
Track risk response
Establish communications

8. Risk Control
Validate mitigation strategies and alternatives
Take corrective action when actual events occur
Assess impact on the project of actions taken (cost, time, resources)
Identify new risks resulting from risk mitigation actions
Ensure that the project plan (including the risk-management plan) is maintained
Ensure change control addresses risks associated with the proposed change
Revise risk register

9. Define Assumptions That Have a Significant Impact on Project Risk

10. Define the Roles and Responsibilities Unique to the Risk Management Function			
Risk Response Tracking Coordinator	Risk Management Team Member	Risk Management Team Member	Risk Management Team Member

11. Define Risk Management Milestones	
Milestone	Date
Risk-management plan approved	
Risk assessment questionnaire tailored to the project	
Risk assessment questionnaire and project planning risk evaluation checklist complete	

Risk management reviews scheduled	

12. Define Risk Rating Scoring Technique (the project will rate each identified risk (e.g., impact score – high, medium, low) based on the likelihood that the risk event will occur and the affect on the project's objectives if the risk event occurs. This will be subjective and based on the experience of those assigned to the project's risk management team).

Default rating/scoring system is as follows:
Impact score may be rated as 1, 3, 5, 7, 9 (1 = very low, 9 = very high)

Probability may be rated as 0.1, 0.3, 0.5, 0.7, 0.9 (0.1 = very low,0. 9 = very high)

13. Establish the Risk Thresholds

Risk priority is determined by calculating the risk score (= Impact * Probability) and then comparing that risk score to priority thresholds. Based on the scoring system, the lowest possible risk score is 1 * 0.1 = .01 and the highest possible risk score is 9 * 0.9 = 8.1

The following priority thresholds will be used to establish risk priority:
Green (low risk) <= 2.5

Yellow (medium risk) between 2.5 and 6.5

Red (high risk) >=6.5

High Risk
The project team develops a full response plan for each item rated as high risk. These risks are watched closely.

Medium Risk
The project team should create a response plan for any medium-risk item where they deem it necessary. However, in general, no response plan is required for medium risk items. Medium risks are monitored on a regular basis.

Low Risk
No action is required for low-risk items except to keep a watch on them as the project progresses. All risk items with a response plan are to be entered into the risk register document.

14. Define Risk Communications

15. Define Risk Tracking Process

16. Project Risk-Management Plan Signatures			
I have reviewed the information contained in the project risk-management plan and agree			
Name	Role	Signature	Date

The signatures above indicate an understanding of the purpose and content of this document by those signing it. By signing this document, they agree to this as the formal project risk-management plan document.

Risk Identification

Risk identification is the process of identifying and documenting the characteristics of the risks that may potentially affect the project.

Essential Ingredients

The following are the essential ingredients that go into risk identification.

- *Enterprise Environmental Factors*

  Enterprise environmental factors refer to factors outside of the project that have or may significantly influence the project's success. Such factors may include but are not limited to organizational culture or customs, governmental or industry standards, human resources or marketplace conditions.

- *Organizational-Process Assets*

  The organization's policies, guidelines, procedures, plans, and/or standards for conducting work are referred to as organizational-process assets. Historical information that represents what the organization has learned from previous projects is also included in this description.

- *Scope Baseline*

  The project-scope statement is the document that details the project's objectives, deliverables, and requirements. The project-scope statement is designed to give everyone concerned with the project a clear impression of what the outcome of the project is intended to produce.

- *Risk-Management Plan*

  Risk-management planning is the process of deciding how to approach and conduct risk-management activities. This is necessary to ensure that the appropriate amount of time and resources is dedicated to the necessary risk-management activities.

- *Activity-Cost Estimates and Supporting Detail*

  Activity-cost estimates are amounts usually stated in monetary units that reflect the cost of the resources needed to complete the project activities. The following represents the necessary supporting detail. A description of the following is required:

  o   work estimated

  o   how the estimate was developed or the basis of the estimate

  o   assumptions made about the estimates or the method used to determine them

  o   constraints, and

  o   stated estimates within ranges.

- *Activity-Duration Estimates*

  Activity-Duration Estimates are assessments of the likely number of work periods that it will take to complete a scheduled activity.

- *Stakeholder Register*

  The result of identifying stakeholders is the production of a stakeholder register and a stakeholder-management strategy. The stakeholder register is a document intended to capture all details related to the identified stakeholders including their identification information, assessment information, and stakeholder classification.

- *Cost-Management Plan*

  The cost-management plan describes how costs are managed. Cost estimating and cost budgeting are included in the creation of the cost-management plan.

- *Schedule-Management Plan*

  Project-time management is concerned with all processes required to ensure that the project is completed on time. This aspect of the project is managed within the context of the schedule-management plan. Activity definition, activity sequencing, activity-resource estimating, activity-duration estimating, and schedule development are included in the creation of the schedule-management plan.

- *Quality-Management Plan*

  The quality-management plan identifies the quality standards that will be adopted by the project. The quality plan describes how the quality policy will be implemented and managed. Quality planning is included in the creation of the quality-management plan.

- *Project Documents*

   Project documents include but are not limited to assumptions log, work performance reports, earned value reports, network diagrams, baselines, and other project information proven to be valuable in identifying risks.

The Method

The following methods may be used in the risk-identification process.

- *Documentation Reviews*

   Documentation reviews is the process of reviewing all of the project-plan documents, assumptions, and historical information from a total project perspective as well as at the individual deliverables or activities level.

   This review helps the project team to identify risks associated with the project's objectives, pay attention to the quality of the plans and look at consistency between plans.

- *Information Gathering Techniques*

   Several techniques are used for information gathering. These techniques include brainstorming, the Delphi technique, interviewing, root cause identification, and strength and weakness analysis. The Delphi technique is similar to brainstorming. The difference is that the people participating in the meeting do not necessarily know each other nor do they have to be located in the same place. They can participate anonymously.

   o *Checklist Analysis*

      The checklist-analysis process is usually developed based on historical information and previous project team experiences.

   o *Assumptions Analysis*

      Assumptions analysis is a process that requires validating assumptions identified and documented during the course of the project-planning process. Assumptions should be accurate, complete and consistent. It is important that assumptions are tested against two factors:

1. the strength of the assumptions or the validity of the assumption, and

2. the consequences that might impact the project if the assumption turns out to be false. All assumptions that are determined to be false should be evaluated and scored just as risks.

- *Diagramming Techniques*

    Cause-and-effect diagrams (Fishbone or Ishikawa diagram), system or process flowcharts, and influence diagrams are the three types of diagramming techniques that are used in risk identification

    o cause-and-effect diagrams, which are sometimes also referred to as Fishbone or Ishikawa diagrams, display the relationship between the causes of the problems and their effects.

    o process flowcharts display the logical steps that outline how elements of a system relate to each other, what actions cause what response or required steps necessary to accomplish an objective.

    o influence diagrams visually depict risks, decisions, uncertainties or impacts, and how they influence each other.

- *Expert Judgment*

    Expert judgment is used to describe the individuals or groups such as stakeholders, practitioners, or groups of people with specialized knowledge or skills in a particular area.

- *SWOT Analysis*

    This is a technique that examines the project from the strengths, weaknesses, opportunities, and threats perspectives. The intent is to increase the breadth of identified risks by including internally generated risks.

The Result

The risk register is a document that contains
- a list of identified risks
- a list of potential responses
- root causes of risks, and
- updated risk categories.

<table>
<tr><td>

STOP TO
COMPLETE
ACTIVITY
</td><td>

Instructions
</td></tr>
</table>

1. Use the details that you compiled in the previous activities to create the risk register for the project.

2. Feel free to use any templates that you may already have in place for your organization.

3. There may be some fields in the risk management template that you may not have be able to complete. Review these fields now to populate the areas that you can given what you just covered in this section.

Qualitative Risk Analysis

Qualitative risk analysis is the process of prioritizing risks for further analysis by combining the probability and impact of occurrence.

Essential Ingredients

The following are essential ingredients that are necessary for qualitative risk analysis.

*   *Organizational-Process Assets*

    The organization's policies, guidelines, procedures, plans, and/or standards for conducting work are referred to as organizational-process assets.

*   *Project-Scope Statement*

    The project-scope statement is the document that details the project's objectives, deliverables and requirements.

*   *Risk-Management Plan*

    Risk-management planning is the process of deciding how to approach and conduct risk-management activities. This is necessary to ensure that the appropriate amount of time and resources is dedicated to the necessary risk-management activities.

*   *Risk Register*

    The risk register is a document that contains

    o   a list of identified risks

    o   a list of potential responses

  o   root causes of risks, and

  o   updated risk categories.

The Method

- *Risk Probability and Impact Assessment*

  The risk probability and impact assessment is used to determine the probability that the risk events identified will occur. This method also determines the effect of the impact of the risk on the project activities including time, scope, quality, and cost. This method helps to identify risks that require aggressive management.

- Probability and Impact Matrix

  Probability and impact values are predefined measurements that are developed to describe what value to place on a risk event. Various tools and techniques used to identify risk may be used to determine values for probability and impact. Examples of such methods are brainstorming or the Delphi technique.

  The qualitative risk assessment process requires that the probability and impact is assessed for every risk identified during the risk-identification process. The outcome of the probability and impact matrix is an overall risk rating for each of the project's identified risks.

- Risk Categorization

  Risk categorization is a tool and technique that is used to determine the effects of risks on the project. The categories of risks determined in the risk management and planning process may be assessed to identify the elements of the project that are affected by risk.

- *Risk-Data-Quality Assessment*

  Risk-data-quality assessment involves determining how useful the quality of the data collected is in evaluating risk. Some of the following may be examined in arriving at this determination

  - the quality of the data used

  - the availability of data that relate to the risks

  - how well the risk is understood

  - the reliability and integrity of the data, and

  - the accuracy of the data

- *Risk-Urgency Assessment*

  Risk urgency is used to determine how the potential risks might occur and determine responses for those risks that may occur in short order. It is recommended that risk triggers be identified, the time to develop and implement a response, and the overall risk rating that should be used to determine how quickly responses are needed.

- *Expert Judgment*

  Expert judgment is used to describe the individuals or groups such as stakeholders, practitioners, or groups of people with specialized knowledge or skills in a particular area.

The Result

The result of the qualitative risk analysis is the risk register. The risk register will be updated with the following information.

- risk ranking (or priority) for the identified risks
- risks grouped by categories
- a list of risks requiring near-term responses
- a list of risks for additional analysis and response
- a watch list of low-priority risks, and
- trends in qualitative-risk-analysis results.

Instructions

1. Use the details that you compiled in the previous activities to update the risk register for the project.

2. Feel free to use any templates that you may already have in place for your organization.

3. There may be some fields in the risk management template that you may not have been able to complete. Review these fields now to populate the areas that you can given what you just covered in this section.

Quantitative Risk Analysis

Quantitative risk analysis is the process of numerically analyzing the effect that the identified risk may have on overall project objectives.

Essential Ingredients

The following are essential ingredients that go into the quantitative risk analysis process.

- *Organizational-Process Assets*

  The organization's policies, guidelines, procedures, plans, and/or standards for conducting work are referred to as organizational-process assets. Historical information that represents what the organization has learned from previous projects is also included in this description.

- *Risk-Management Plan*

  Risk-management planning is the process of deciding how to approach, and conduct risk-management activities. This is necessary to ensure that the appropriate amount of time and resources is dedicated to the necessary risk-management activities.

- *Risk Register*

  The risk register is a document that contains the following

  o a list of identified risks

  o a list of potential responses

  o root causes of risks, and

  o updated risk categories

- *Cost-Management Plan*

  The cost-management plan describes how costs are managed. Cost estimating and cost budgeting are included in the creation of the cost-management plan.

- *Schedule-Management Plan*

  Project-time management is concerned with all processes required to ensure that the project is completed on time. This aspect of the project is managed within the context of the schedule-management plan. Activity definition, activity sequencing, activity-resource estimating, activity-duration estimating, and schedule development are included in the creation of the schedule-management plan.

The Method

- *Expert Judgment*

  Expert judgment is used to describe the individuals or groups such as stakeholders, practitioners, or groups of people with specialized knowledge or skills in a particular area.

- *Data Gathering and Representation Techniques*

  Data-gathering techniques include interviewing techniques, probability distributions, and expert judgment.

  o *Interviewing*

  In this instance, the project team, stakeholders, and/or subject matter experts are engaged in discussions and are asked to share their experiences on past projects that used the types of technology and processes that are expected to be used on the current project. The decisions that the interviewees make regarding the risk ranges and criteria that they place on certain risk categories are documented.

  o *Probability Distributions*

  Continuous probability distributions are commonly used in quantitative risk analysis.

  o *Expert Judgment*

  Expert judgment is used to describe the individuals or groups such as stakeholders, practitioners, or groups of people with specialized knowledge or skills in a particular area.

- *Quantitative Risk Analysis and Modeling Techniques*

  Sensitivity analysis, expected-monetary-value analysis, decision-tree analysis and modeling, and simulation are included as a part of this tool and technique.

  o *Sensitivity Analysis*

  This is a quantitative method of analyzing the potential impact of risk events on the project. All of the uncertain elements are examined at their baseline values to determine which risk event(s) have the greatest potential for impact.

  o *Expected Monetary Value*

  Expected-monetary-value analysis is a statistical technique that calculates the average anticipated impact of the decision.

Expected monetary value is calculated by multiplying the probability of the risk by the impact and then adding both values together.

o   *Decision-Tree Analysis*

Decision trees are diagrams that show the sequence of interrelated decisions and the expected results of choosing one alternative over the other. Decision trees are usually used for risk events associated with time or cost.

o   *Modeling and Simulation*

Modeling and simulation are tools and techniques that are often used for schedule risk analysis, and cost analysis.

Modeling makes it possible to translate the potential risks at specific points in the project into their impacts to determine the effect on the project objectives.

The Result

The result of quantitative risk analysis is updates to the risk register. The risk register will be updated with the following information

- risk ranking (or priority) for the identified risks

- risks grouped by categories

- a list of risks requiring near-term responses

- a list of risks for additional analysis and response

- a watch list of low-priority risks, and

- trends in qualitative-risk-analysis results.

 Instructions

1. Use the details that you compiled in the previous activities to update the risk register for the project.

2. Feel free to use any templates that you may already have in place for your organization.

3. There may be some fields in the risk management template that you may not have be able to complete. Review these fields now to populate the areas that you can given what you just covered in this section.

Risk-Response Planning

Risk-response planning is the final component of risk that is included in the project-planning process. Risk-response planning is concerned with developing options and actions to enhance opportunities and reduce the threat of risk on project objectives.

Essential Ingredients

There are two essential ingredients that should be considered in risk-response planning. They are the risk-management plan and the risk register.

* *Risk-Management Plan*

    Risk-management planning is the process of deciding how to approach and conduct risk-management activities. This is necessary to ensure that the appropriate amount of time and resources is dedicated to the necessary risk-management activities.

* *Risk Register*

    The risk register is a document that contains the following

    o   a list of identified risks

    o   a list of potential responses

    o   root causes of risks, and

    o   updated risk categories

The Method

* *Strategies for Negative Risks or Threats*

    There are three strategies that may be considered when dealing with negative risks or threats to project objectives. They are avoid, transfer, and/or mitigate.

    o   *Avoid*

        Avoid means to evade the risk, eliminate the cause of the risk event or change the project plan to protect the project objectives from the risk event.

    o   *Transfer*

        Transferring the risk does not eliminate the risk; it merely moves the risk and the consequences of that risk to a third party. Insurance is one form of risk transfer.

o   Mitigate

The purpose of mitigation is to attempt to reduce the probability of a risk event and its impact to an acceptable level.

- *Strategies for Positive Risks or Opportunities*

There are three strategies that may be considered when dealing with positive risks or opportunities. They are exploit, share, and/or enhance.

o   *Exploit*

Exploiting a risk event is a strategy that may be used when positive risks are identified, and the intention is to ensure that these risks occur on the project.

o   *Share*

Sharing is a strategy where the risk is assigned to a third party who is best able to bring about the opportunity that the risk event presents.

o   *Enhance*

Enhancing entails watching for and enhancing risk triggers and identifying the root causes of risks to help enhance impacts or probability.

- *Contingent Response Strategy*

Contingency planning describes a process to deal with the risks as they occur. Contingency planning does not necessarily attempt to reduce the risk events or its impact. Contingency planning recognizes that a risk may occur, and seeks to have a plan in place to address the anticipated risk event.

- *Expert Judgment*

Expert judgment is used to describe the individuals or groups such as stakeholders, practitioners, or groups of people with specialized knowledge or skills in a particular area.

The Result

The following are the results of the risk response plan.
- *Updates to Risk Register*

The risk register will be updated with the following information:

- o a list of identified risks including their descriptions, the work-breakdown structure elements that they impact, categories, root causes, and how the risk impacts the project objectives

- o risk owners and their responsibility

- o risk triggers

- o response plans, and strategies, including the steps to take to implement the strategy

- o cost and schedule activities needed to implement risk responses

- o contingency reserves for cost and time

- o contingency plans

- o fall-back plans

- o list of residual and secondary risks, and

- o probabilistic analysis of the project and other outputs of the qualitative and quantitative risk analysis process.

- *Risk-Related Contractual Agreements*

  The use of risk strategies such as transference or sharing may require the purchase of services and/or items from third parties. As such, there may be a need to prepare the appropriate contracts to secure the necessary services or items.

- *Updates to Project-Management Plan*

  Requested changes to the project-management plan and its subsidiary plans that result from the risk-response planning process are processed and actioned through the integrated change control process.

- *Project Document Updates*

  The project documents that may be updated include but are not limited to assumptions log updates and technical documentation updates.

STOP TO COMPLETE ACTIVITY

Instructions

1. Use the details that you compiled in the previous activities to complete the respective updates based on the results of the risk response plan.

2. Feel free to use any templates that you may already have in place for your organization.

3. There may be some fields in the risk management template that you may not have be able to complete. Review these fields now to populate the areas that you can given what you just covered in this section.

Plan Procurements

Plan procurements is the final section to cover in the project-planning process group. Plan procurements describes the process of documenting project purchasing decisions, specifying the approach, and identifying potential sellers. Plan procurements identifies the project needs that can best be or must be met by acquiring products, services, or results outside of the project organization, versus those project needs that can be accomplished through the efforts of the project team.

Essential Ingredients

The following are essential ingredients that go into plan procurements.

- *Enterprise Environmental Factors*

    Enterprise environmental factors refer to factors outside of the project that have or may significantly influence the project's success. Such factors may include but are not limited to organizational culture or customs, governmental or industry standards, human resources or marketplace conditions.

- *Organizational-Process Assets*

    The organization's policies, guidelines, procedures, plans, and/or standards for conducting work are referred to as organizational-process assets. Historical information that represents what the organization has learned from previous projects is also included in this description.

- *Scope Baseline*

    The project-scope statement is the document that details the project's objectives, deliverables, and requirements. The project-scope statement is designed to give everyone concerned with the project a clear impression of what the outcome of the project is intended to produce.

- *Requirements Documentation*

    Requirements documentation describes the connection between individual requirements and the business need for the project. Components of requirements documentation may include but are not limited to business need for the project or product, functional and non-functional requirements, quality requirements, acceptable criteria as well as impacts in other entities, and other organizational areas.

- *Teaming Agreements*

  Teaming agreements are legal contractual agreements between two or more entities to form a partnership or joint venture or some other arrangement as defined by both parties. These agreements define the roles for the buyer and the seller. As such, whenever teaming agreements are in place on a project, the roles of the buyer and the seller are predefined. Issues such as scope of work, completion requirements, and other critical issues are generally predefined.

- *Risk Register*

  The risk register is a document that contains the following

  o   a list of identified risks

  o   a list of potential responses

  o   root causes of risks, and

  o   updated risk categories.

- *Risk-Related Contractual Decisions*

  The use of risk strategies such as transference or sharing may require the purchase of services and/or items from third parties. As such, there may be a need to prepare the appropriate contracts to secure the necessary services or items. Such decisions may include insurance and other services that are prepared to specify each parties' responsibility for specific risks.

- *Activity-Resource Requirements*

  Activity-resources requirement describes the types and quantity of resources required for each scheduled activity.

- *Project Schedule*

  The project schedule determines the start and finish dates for each project activity in addition to the resource assignments. Once the project schedule is signed off and approved, it becomes the baseline for the remainder of the project.

- *Activity-Cost Estimates and Supporting Detail*

  Activity-cost estimates are amounts usually stated in monetary units that reflect the cost of the resources needed to complete the project activities. A description of the following is required:

  o work estimated

  o outline of how the estimate was developed or the basis of the estimate

  o assumptions made about the estimates or the method used to determine them

  o constraints, and

  o stated estimates within ranges.

- *Cost-Performance Baseline*

  The cost baseline is a time-phased budget that is used as a basis for measuring, monitoring, and controlling overall cost performance on the project. The cost baseline is developed by adding the costs of the work-breakdown structure according to time periods.

The Method

The following method is required for plan procurements:

- *Make-or-Buy Analysis*

  Make-or-buy analysis investigates whether it is more cost effective to buy the products or services as opposed to producing the goods or services needed for the project.

- *Contract Types*

  Contract types are divided into three categories: fixed price or lump sum, cost reimbursable, and/or time and materials.

  o *Fixed price or lump sum*

     Fixed price contracts set a specific, firm price for the goods or services rendered. The seller assumes the biggest risk in these kinds of contracts as it relates to risks of increasing costs, nonperformance, or other problems. The seller typically builds in the cost of the risk to the contract price as a counter to these unforeseen risks.

o *Cost Reimbursable*

In cost reimbursable contracts, the seller is reimbursed by the buyer for all of the costs the seller takes on during the project. Cost reimbursable contracts carry the highest risk to the buyer because the total costs are uncertain.

o *Time and Material*

Time and material contracts are a cross between fixed price and cost reimbursable contracts. The buyer assumes the biggest risk in these types of contracts as the full amount of the material cost is not known at the time that the contract is awarded.

• *Expert Judgment*

Expert judgment is used to describe the individuals or groups such as stakeholders, practitioners, or groups of people with specialized knowledge or skills in a particular area.

The Result

• *Procurement-Management Plan*

The procurement-management plan describes how the procurement processes will be managed throughout the project. This might include information such as contract type, procurement documents, and lead times for purchases. Plan purchases and acquisitions and plan contracting are included in the procurement-management plan.

• *Procurement Statement of Work*

A procurement statement of work describes the procurement item in sufficient detail to allow prospective sellers to determine if they are capable of providing the required products, services, or results. The procurement statement of work is developed from the project-scope baseline and defines only that portion of the project scope that is to be included in the related contract. Information in the procurement statement of work may include specifications on the quantity desired, performance data, work location, and other requirements.

• *Make or Buy Decisions*

This is a document that outlines the decisions made during the decision to determine the goods and/or services that will be produced by the organization versus the ones that will be purchased.

- *Requested Changes*

  Requested changes may come about as a result of the plan purchases and acquisitions process. Those changes should be administered through the integrated change-control process.

- *Procurement Documents*

  Procurement documents are structured by the buyer and are used to solicit proposals from prospective sellers. Terms such as *bid, tender,* or *quotation* are generally used when the seller-selection decision will be based on price. Terms such as *proposal* are generally used when other considerations such as technical capability or technical approach are the important considerations. Common procurement terms may include *request for information* (RFI), *invitation for bid* (IFB), *request for proposal* (RFP), *request for quotation* (RFQ), and *tender notice* among others.

  Procurement documents should clearly state the method that the seller should use to format and submit their responses as well as a clear description of the work that is requested. Procurement documents should be prepared by the buyer to assure as accurate and complete response as possible from all potential bidders.

- *Source-Selection Criteria*

  Selection criteria are developed and used to rate or score seller proposals and are often included as a part of the procurement documents. In some cases, selection criteria may be limited to purchase price (including the cost of the item and all ancillary expenses such as delivery.) In other instances, additional criteria are used, some of which are presented below:

  o   an understanding of the needs of the project as documented in the contract statement of work

  o   technical ability of the vendor and their proposed team

  o   experience on projects of similar size and scope, including references

  o   project management approach

  o   management approach

  o   financial stability and capacity, and

  o   intellectual and proprietary rights.

Instructions

1. Use the details that you compiled in the previous activities to complete the procurement plan.

2. Feel free to use any templates that you may already have in place for your organization.

Procurement Plan Template

Some fields include instruction on how to populate the document

Project Name:	
Prepared by:	
Date:	

1. Procurement Statement (describe in general terms what products or services are being considered for procurement)

2. Estimated Cost

Provide an estimated total cost of all procurements in this project. Include confidence limits for your estimates (e.g., plus/minus dollars or percent of estimate). Example: $1,444.000 +/- 40%

3. Vendor Selection

Describe what approach the project team will take to select a product or vendor (e.g., Request for Information (RFI), Request for Proposal (RFP)).

4. Procurement Definition

Describe in specific terms what items will be procured and under what conditions

5. Selection Process and Criteria

Describe the selection process. List and describe selection criteria.

6. Procurement Team

List all stakeholders who are involved in the procurement process along with contact information and description of procurement role

Name	Phone/e-mail	Procurement Role

7. Contract Type

Document what type of contract(s) will be used and the actions required to initiate the contract.

8. Contract Standards

Provide the standards for documentation that will be used for each contract

9. Vendor Management
Describe what steps the project team will take to ensure that the vendor provides all of the products and/or services (and only the products and services) that were agreed-upon and that appropriate levels of quality are maintained.

10. Project Procurement Plan Signatures

I have reviewed the information contained in the project procurement plan and agree

Name	Role	Signature	Date

The signatures above indicate an understanding of the purpose and content of this document by those signing it. By signing this document, they agree to this as the formal project procurement plan document.

THE FOUR-STEP COMBO

Step 3

Chapter 6
Development and Implementation

After studying this chapter, you should be able to

- outline the terms and definitions used in the communication process.

- list and describe the barriers to effective communication.

- list and describe the ways that expectations are typically created.

- describe the four dimensions of credibility and explain the importance to the success of the learning program.

- list and describe the basic principles that should be present in all outlines.

- list and describe the three types of emphasis in writing and explain why this method should be used.

- define psychological emphasis. Explain three ways that psychological emphasis may be achieved.

- list and describe the various types of support methods that are used in the area of evidence and elaboration.

As you read this chapter, be sure that you understand the following terms and ideas.

- Source
- Channel
- Decoding
- Internal Noise
- Attitudes

- Receiver
- Feedback
- Nonverbal
- Perception
- Values

- Message
- Encoding
- External Noise
- Beliefs
- Noise

- Expertise
- Dynamism
- Projecting Credibility
- Subordination
- Verbal Emphasis

- Trustworthiness
- Creating a Climate
- Simplicity
- Progression
- Evidence and Elaboration

- Polish
- Previewing the Content
- Coordination
- Symbolization
- Psychological Emphasis

The weekend's over. It's Monday morning and you're back to work. You check your calendar, only to be reminded that the meeting with the boss is scheduled to begin in the next five minutes. How could you have forgotten? You peruse the agenda and notice that it includes an update from you.

You hurriedly gather your papers and working documents and arrive at the meeting seconds before it begins. The boss welcomes you and once again congratulates you on your efforts and achievements. Then the surprise announcement is made. Sign-off is obtained on the design document and project plan, without the need for edits! You smile shyly and secretly begin to sweat nervous bullets.

Discussion ensues. The meeting concludes. You go back to your desk and think about what you need to do to begin working on developing the learner and facilitator guides.

Overview

Writing the learner and facilitator guides requires a thorough understanding of oral and written communication and well-honed skills in business writing. While you have experience writing learner and facilitator guides, your previous projects were nowhere near as high profile as this one. Upon review of the writing templates that you used in the past, you find them to be inappropriate for this project.

Where do you begin? Fortunately, you were able to arrange a meeting with a communications expert who will assist you with moving your design document to development. Your one-on-one coaching with the communications expert will include a review of the following items presented below, which are presented in greater detail in this chapter.

- The communication process
- Barriers to effective communication
- Creating positive expectations

- Fitting the message together
- Assessing key ideas
- Evidence and elaboration

It is important that the use of the learner and facilitator guides meet learner expectations as well as the organization's performance and business outcomes. Soliciting assistance with this aspect of the project will go a long way in realizing this goal.

Objective for the Automated Sales-Management Training

The automated sales-management training is designed to teach learners to accurately navigate through the respective screens to achieve performance targets for appointments and generate corresponding sales from prospect calls.

Effective communication is essential in realizing the training objective. Effective communication allows us to create a degree of accurate understanding among learners. The degree of understanding created and the degree to which learners respond appropriately to the message is the key measure of success. This section discusses the essentials required for developing the learner and facilitator guide. Some information presented may also be used as tips when facilitating the session.

The Communication Process

Terms	Definitions
Source	The one who begins the communication through verbal or nonverbal means. Other names for the source include the encoder, the speaker, or the writer.
Receiver	The one to whom the source's verbal and/or nonverbal communication is directed. Other names for the receiver include the decoder, listener, or the audience.
Message	The information or product of the source's purpose, which is coded into symbols and/or language and expressed through verbal and/or nonverbal means.
Channel	The medium through which a message is transmitted.
Feedback	The receiver's response to the source's message. Feedback indicates how well the source is communicating the message.

Encoding	A process involving selecting a means of expressing and transforming ideas into appropriate symbols and/or language.
Decoding	The receiver's interpretation of the message based on background, education, and future expectations.
Nonverbal	The use of hand gestures, posture, eye contact, vocal tone, and personal distance to emphasize or complement oral communication.
External Noise	Any external interference in the environment that prevents the message from being accurately encoded or decoded.
Internal Noise	Any internal interference in one's mind that prevents the message from being accurately encoded or decoded.

Barriers to Effective Communication

The barriers to communication outlined below for review include perception, beliefs, attitudes, values, and noise.

Perception
No two people perceive the same event in the same way. The images in people's heads are formed through the process of perception. Perception allows people to take in, organize, and make sense of information from the world around them. The differences in people's perceptions are natural and inevitable.

Beliefs
Our individual field of reference is a composite of our unique beliefs, attitudes, and values. A belief may be described as a conviction that something is true or false or that it is probable or improbable. A conviction may be based on evidence, experience, faith, or confidence. Some beliefs may be based on false evidence, incomplete data, or may be distorted by emotion; nevertheless, these beliefs play an important role in perception and communication.

Attitudes
Attitudes affect our frame of reference. Our attitudes may be described as our inclinations or tendencies to respond positively or negatively to persons, objects, or situations. Attitudes are always directed toward something. Attitudes may be triggered by beliefs, as they tend to be a predisposition for and

against objects and issues. People change attitudes when they realize that the attitude is no longer useful or appropriate.

Values
Values are our general notions of what is good or bad or what is preferred or rejected. Values serve as the foundation for beliefs and attitudes and are highly resistant to change. It is important for the instructional designer as well as the facilitator to develop an awareness of the nature and strength of the beliefs, attitudes, and values of the learners. Failure to do so may lead to frequent breakdowns in creating meaning.

Noise
The term *noise* is used by communication theorists to refer to any kind of distortion or disruption of the communication process. This may include internal and/or external noise.

Creating Positive Expectations

Just the appearance of a learner guide or other course material or literature may result in immediate expectations being formed. Speculation is made about the message even before it is communicated. Speculation is also made about the source of the message, the speaker or the writer, and what that person's motives and intentions may be.

As such, it makes sense for the instructional designer to create the most appropriate and positive expectation early in the communication—at the point of developing facilitator notes in the facilitator guide. Expectations are typically created in at least three different ways: projecting credibility, creating a climate, and previewing the content.

Projecting Credibility

Audiences tend to draw conclusions about the credibility of the learning program very early in the communication process. This includes assumptions about the facilitator, as well as the content and appearance of the learner guide.

High credibility is the ability of the facilitator or the instructional designer to inspire faith. Expertise, trustworthiness, polish, and dynamism are four dimensions of credibility.

Expertise

The degree to which the facilitator or the instructional designer is informed about a particular topic affects his or her credibility. Generally, someone with high credibility has had training and/or experience relevant to the topic being discussed. This person is capable of displaying this competence. Citing respected sources of information and using illustrations that reflect upon the personal understanding of the topic help to convey such expertise. All of this must be taken into consideration in not only developing the learner and facilitator guide, but also in selecting the facilitator for the session.

Trustworthiness

Credibility is enhanced when an instructional designer appears to be sincere and unbiased. This impression can be created by being fair in using facts and careful reasoning and by avoiding language that conveys undue emotionalism. Careful thought and consideration must be placed in this area when writing the learner guides as well as facilitator notes for the facilitator guide.

Polish

Another factor affecting credibility is the polish and professionalism that the instructional designer projects in the written message. The instructional designer and the facilitator must strive for professionalism where close attention is paid to details in both the written and/oral presentation of the material. These details create positive first impressions in the learner's mind.

Dynamism

Credibility is also affected by personal dynamism—the tendency to be outgoing, friendly, and articulate. These attributes are particularly important for the facilitator to demonstrate authentically to the learner. The friendly, enthusiastic, yet sincere message is likely to be well received.

Creating a Climate

The climate of the communication situation may project clues to the audience. A facilitator who warms up with an icebreaker that involves a joke or a humorous story also creates a certain climate. The same principle can be used in written messages. The language and presentation of the learner guide can create an upbeat climate.

Previewing the Content

An old adage of public speaking says, "Tell them what you are going to tell them, tell them, and then tell them what you just told them." The first part of that three-step advice is what we refer to as previewing the content.

Previewing the content can be general or quite specific. The general preview sets the stage for what is to come. The specific-content preview includes details. Any communication situation begins with certain mental expectations. It is very important that the instructional designer builds both the learner and facilitator guide with content preview as a lead-in to each section, unit, and module. Simply telling the learner what is coming next is one of the simplest ways of improving the chances that the learner will get and use the message as intended.

Previewing the content helps to create realistic expectations in the learner's mind. By doing this, misconceptions are reduced and the accuracy of communication is improved.

Fitting the Message Together

An outline is a crucially important working tool. Outlines categorize information and separate main ideas from subordinate ones. All forms of outline share certain basic principles. These principles are simplicity, coordination, subordination, progression, and symbolization.

Simplicity

When an outline is used as a tool to organize a message, it should assist rather than confuse the learner. Each line should represent a single bit of information. This information may be written out in full sentence. Often, a phrase or key word is very useful.

Coordination

The principle of coordination means that all points within a subdivision must be logically related. For example, if the facilitator is discussing the benefits of using the automated sales-management system to obtain calls from the prospect list and schedule appointments, the following benefits may be covered:

a) A list is automatically generated by the system for the sales officer's convenience.

b) Having a prospect list in advance allows the sales officer to profile the customer prior to the call and save time in the long run.

c) The system's built-in features allow the sales officer to review and/or record notes specific to the customer.

d) Forfeiture of all bonus compensation is a penalty for failure to use the automated sales-management system.

Item D is the only item under "benefits" that is out of place. Item D does not offer a positive incentive but rather warns the sales officer to use the automated sales-management system to avoid forfeiting compensation. This item should be placed elsewhere.

Subordination

The principle of subordination refers to the way a main idea is divided into subordinate parts. Each entry in an outline should be directly related to the preceding category.

Progression

The parts of the learning content must be arranged in some logical pattern to show progression from one point to another. It is important when writing that the instructional designer stays consistent within the pattern selected.

Symbolization

Symbolization is the way to denote coordination, subordination, and progression of the learning content. Typically, a combination of roman numbers, capital letters, and lowercase letters may be used. If any heading is to be subdivided, several subheadings should follow. For example, point A may be followed by numbers 1 and 2. Using the outline developed in the design document guides the instructional designer in clarifying key points and sequencing them in a systematic format.

Accessing Key Ideas

In any message, there are certain ideas or bits of information that are more important than others. It is important that the instructional designer and the facilitator point out to the learner the bits of information that are more important. Important information should receive a position of prominence. Key ideas should be asserted in obvious ways that jump out at the learner. There are three types of emphasis in writing: verbal, visual, and psychological. Each of these may be used to point to the key idea of the message.

Verbal Emphasis

An important use of verbal emphasis is to provide word cues that indicate when a key idea is coming. For example, the facilitator may say, "The most important aspect of the automated sales-management system is ...," or, "This last part is particularly important," or, "Please read these instructions carefully." These overt cues to the learner may be used in either written or oral communication.

The second type of verbal emphasis is the use of repetition. When a key idea is repeated several times (preferably phrased a little differently each time), the learner gets the idea that this is, in fact, an important bit of information.

Visual Emphasis

Several types of visual emphasis may be used to help the facilitator and the learner skim through the message and get the important ideas. These visual techniques include the following.

- Enumeration – 1, 2, 3; or I, II, III; or a, b, c
- Listing
- Numerals
- Letters
- Asterisks or stars
- Hyphens
- Bullets
- Capitalization
- Underlining
- Borders
- Type variation
- Graphics
- Shading or highlighting
- Margins
- White spaces

Paragraphs in learner guides should be short. Learners prefer to read information presented in manageable bits.

Psychological Emphasis

Using psychological principles to point out information relates closely to the way information is arranged in the message. Psychological emphasis may be achieved in the following three ways: order, space, and freshness.

Order
When information is clearly pointed out to the learner in an ordered format, the learner can anticipate what is coming next and remember what is already said. This form of psychological emphasis helps the learner to separate key ideas from the extraneous. Strong use of content preview and clear arrangement applies here.

Space
Space, in terms of psychological emphasis, refers to the relative amount of space devoted to a particular topic. For example, if the facilitator spends ten minutes on the topic of the benefits of the automated sales-management system and only one minute on the functionality, the learner may psychologically determine that the benefits of the automated system are more important than the functionality.

Freshness
Psychological emphasis may be achieved through fresh approaches, a catchy idea, or a particularly innovative notion.

Evidence and Elaboration

Once key ideas are pointed out and presented in a learner guide or facilitated session, these ideas need to be adequately supported. The commonly used support methods outlined below include details or explanations, comparisons, analogies or metaphors, examples, definitions, statistics, charts, graphs, and other visual supports.

Details or Explanations
This type of support simply restates or explains in different words what the key idea asserts.

Comparisons, Analogies, or Metaphors
An appropriate analogy or metaphor may communicate a concept or idea far more clearly and interestingly than a mere explanation can. Often, analogies are short narratives or stories.

Examples
Illustrations or examples, especially those from experiences, are good sources of support for key ideas. They also give credibility to the instructional designer as well as the facilitator.

Definitions
Defining important terms may be useful to support key ideas and clarify specialized terms that the learner may not know. The facilitator is advised to take time to define terms that the learners may be unfamiliar with to ensure that the audience remains engaged.

Statistics
It is important that the instructional designer understands statistics and their implications before using them. The instructional designer should know how the statistics are derived and how to interpret them. The learner's ability to understand statistical information must be considered.

Charts, Graphs, and Other Visual Supports
Visual displays can and should be used in conjunction with many kinds of support to enhance the learning experience.

Facilitator Manual

The following information is included in the facilitator's manual.
- Diagrams for recommended room set-up and facilities required
- Equipment and supplies required
- Copy of participant's manual and/or handouts

Concluding Developing and Implementing Course Material

Validation

Once the course material is designed and developed, the next step is to test the prototype and launch the course. Validation is a pilot or field test of the course and is conducted before the learning program is rolled out. In the case of the automated sales-management training program, the prototype was tested on a sample group of sales officers randomly selected from another division of the organization.

The course was validated in the areas of content, process, and materials.

Validation Criteria	Example of Questions Asked
Content	• Was there a clear link between the content and the objectives? • Was the information relevant to the job? • Was the learning content relevant to the tasks to be performed? • Was the flow of the information presented in the learning content clearly presented? • Was the information presented detailed? • Was learning reinforced throughout the program?
Process	• Were the examples and/or analogies relevant? • Could this information be applied to the job? • Did the presentation method help you to learn the content? • Did the application method help you to understand how to perform the job? • Were the analogies and/or examples sufficient to result in comprehension of the learning content?
Materials	• Were the manuals, job aids, and performance checklists adequate, useful, and applicable to the job? • Was the appearance of the materials easy to read? • Was the material presented in the technical learner guide (inclusive of screen shots) easy to navigate?

Relevant changes were made based on the feedback. The program was successfully launched in accordance with the timeline communicated in the communication management plan.

The following chapter explains the project's executing, monitoring, and control processes that were used to ensure success.

Applying to the Next Project

Discussion Questions

1. What are the terms and definitions used in the communication process?

2. What are the barriers to effective communication?

3. In which ways are expectations typically created?

4. What are the four dimensions of credibility?

5. Why is establishing credibility essential to the success of the learning program?

6. What are the basic principles that should be present in all outlines in oral and written communication?

7. What are the three types of emphasis in writing?

8. Why should the method of creating emphasis in writing be used?

9. What is psychological emphasis?

10. What are three ways that psychological emphasis may be achieved in oral and written communication?

11. What are the various types of support methods that are used in the area of evidence and elaboration as it relates to oral and written communication?

Chapter 7
Executing, Monitoring, and Controlling

After studying this chapter, you should be able to

- define project execution and explain its importance.

- list and describe the multiple actions required to be completed as a part of project execution.

- explain the purpose of quality assurance and describe what quality assurance entails.

- explain how team members may be acquired and describe what this process entails.

- explain what developing the project team entails, explain why it is important to develop the team, and state who is responsible for project-team development.

- explain why distributing project information is important, how is it done and how the lessons-learned activity fits into the overall process.

- explain the purpose for monitoring and controlling the project.

- describe the activities that take place in monitoring and controlling the project plan.

- explain the purpose of integrated change control and describe the activities that take place in this area.

- explain the purpose of scope verification and scope control and describe what takes place in each of these areas.

- explain why monitoring and controlling the project schedule is important.

- explain why it is important to monitor and control cost in a project.

- state the purpose of performing quality control when monitoring and controlling the project.

- describe the purpose of performance reporting as a part of monitoring and controlling the project plan.

- explain the activities that take place as a part of risk monitoring and controlling.

- explain the activities that take place as a part of contract administration.

As you read this chapter, be sure that you understand the following terms and ideas.

- Perform Quality Assurance
- Distribute Project Information
- Perform Integrated Change Control

- Schedule Control
- Performance Reporting

- Acquire the Project Team
- Manage Stakeholder Expectations
- Verifying Scope

- Cost Control
- Monitoring and Controlling Risk

- Develop the Project Team
- Conduct Procurements
- Monitor and Control Project Work
- Controlling Scope
- Quality Control
- Administering Procurements

You prepare to chair your first project team meeting. While you wait for the meeting to begin, you conduct a high-level review of the agenda in your mind and think about what you intend to discuss with the group. Your plan is to do the following

- o Welcome the group to the meeting.

- o Inform the group that the Automated Sales-Management Training Project is at the execution stage.

- o Outline the following tasks that must be completed as a part of project execution:

    - o Acquiring the project team

    - o Developing the project team (this is an ongoing process)

    - o Distributing information

    - o Requesting seller responses

    - o Selecting sellers

    - o Performing quality assurance (this is an ongoing process)

- o Inform the group of the tasks that are a part of project execution that are completed to-date

    - o Acquired project team

    - o Requested seller responses

    - o Selected sellers

- o Inform the team that the purpose of the meeting is to distribute and discuss the information that relates to the project.

Your name is announced. It's your turn to speak. You thank the team for attending the meeting and communicate the message above that you spent the last five minutes formulating in your head. After expressing excitement that the project is nearing completion, you proceed to review the following items:

- o Project milestones included in the project scope document

- o Project schedule, highlighting dates of critical importance

- o The communication schedule included in the project communication plan

Given that launch date for the training course is fast approaching, you spend considerable time discussing the communication schedule outlined in the project communication plan with particular emphasis on the following items.

- o Purpose for the communication events

- o   Audience
- o   Channel
- o   Responsibility for communicating the message
- o   Delivery date

You gain consensus and team buy-in for the roles that they will play to ensure a successful project launch. You conclude by updating the team on the following:

- o   the vendor's progress with developing and testing the automated sales-management training database.

- o   the vendor's progress with developing the technical lesson guides, inclusive of screen shots and step-by-step instructions for use of system functionality.

- o   your progress in developing the learner and facilitator guides with instructions for individual and group activities (inclusive of non-systems based learning checks, final assessments, and product sales supplemental reading materials).

The meeting ends and you and the team go back to work.

Overview

You have created the project plan and obtained sign-off. Sign-off authorizes work on the project plan to begin. Execution involves carrying out the work outlined in the project plan. Project execution requires mobilizing all committed project resources and ensuring that these resources carry out their intended activities. The project manager and the project team are required to perform multiple actions to ensure the project's success. Some of these actions include acquiring and developing the project team, distributing project information, obtaining seller's request, selecting sellers, and performing quality assurance. All of these tasks are described in greater detail in this chapter. All processes should be considered, although not necessarily performed as a part of the project executing and monitoring and controlling. The decision on the processes to be performed is based on the size and complexity of the project.

Perform Quality Assurance

Quality assurance is performed as an important part of project execution. Quality assurance is the process of auditing the quality requirements and the results from quality control measurement to ensure that appropriate quality standards and operational definitions are used.

Acquire the Project Team

Acquiring the project team is one of the essential requirements for project execution. Project-team members may be selected from inside or outside of the organization. The project manager may be responsible for ensuring that the resources are available and skilled in the project activities to which they are assigned. The project manager may be required to negotiate with others for the best resources.

Develop the Project Team

With the team in place, the next step is to develop the team. This requires creating the right environment to facilitate the team developing into an effective, functioning, coordinated group. Teams that work well together tend to perform at greater levels of efficiency and effectiveness. It is important that the project manager demonstrates the management and leadership skills necessary to develop the team. These skills include organization, problem solving, negotiation, communication, and the ability to empathize and relate well to others.

Motivation and incentive are essential to developing the team. The project manager would be required to provide motivation, reward, and recognition to keep the team performing as a cohesive body. The project manager may also initiate ongoing team building activities to promote, develop, and maintain team synergy.

Distribute Project Information

Stakeholders must be able to access information about the project in a timely manner. This can be achieved through status reports, project meetings, and the like. Status reports inform the stakeholders about where the project is as it relates to the project schedule, budget, and other components of the project plan. Status reports also outline what the project team has accomplished to date. Such accomplishments might include milestones completed to date, percentage of schedule completion as well as outstanding work to be completed.

The communication management plan is active in this process, and is used as an important tool to report the project teams' progress.

Manage Stakeholder Expectations

Managing stakeholder expectations involves managing communications to satisfy stakeholder requirements and resolve possible issues as they arise. Managing stakeholder expectations helps to increase the probability of project success by ensuring that the stakeholders understand the project benefits and risks.

Conduct Procurements

The process of obtaining seller responses, selecting a seller, and awarding a contract is referred to as conducting procurements. Bidder conferences are meetings between the buyer, and prospective seller prior to the submittal of a bid or proposal. These meetings are designed to ensure that all prospective sellers have a clear and common understanding of the technical and contractual requirements that relate to the procurement process. Bidder conferences, proposal evaluations (where selection will be made on previously defined weighted criteria), independent estimates, expert judgment, advertising, internet search, and procurement negotiations are all methods that may be used to conduct procurements.

Monitoring and Controlling Project Work

Monitoring and controlling project work involves tracking, reviewing, and regulating processes to meet performance objectives outlined in the project-management plan. This includes performing integrated change control, verifying scope, controlling scope, controlling schedule, controlling cost, controlling quality, performance reporting, monitoring and controlling risk, and administering procurements.

Perform Integrated Change Control

The project-management plan, the project-scope statement, and other deliverables are maintained by carefully and continuously managing approved changes either by rejecting or accepting them. This describes the process of integrated change control.

Verifying Scope

Scope verification is primarily concerned with formally accepting completed project deliverables.

Controlling Scope

Controlling the scope includes all of the processes involved in monitoring the status of the project and product scope and managing changes to the scope baseline. This includes ensuring that all requested changes, recommended corrective action, or preventive actions are processed through the integrated change-control process.

Schedule Control

Controlling the scope involves the process of determining the current status of the project schedule, influencing the factors that create schedule changes, determining whether the project schedule has changed, and managing actual changes as they occur.

Cost Control

Updating the project budget and monitoring expenses are a part of controlling costs. Cost control also involves analyzing how the project funds are used in relation to the work that is being accomplished.

Quality Control

Quality control measures are performed throughout the entire project and are intended to identify causes of poor process or product quality and recommend and/or take action to eliminate them.

Performance Reporting

Performance reporting involves periodically collecting and analyzing the baseline and comparing the results to actual data. Once the project's progress and performance is understood the necessary information is communicated to the relevant stakeholders.

Monitoring and Controlling Risk

Monitoring and controlling risk includes implementing risk-response plans, tracking identified risks, monitoring residual risks, identifying new risks, and evaluating the effectiveness of the risk plan throughout the project.

Administering Procurements

A part of administering the contract involves monitoring the vendor's performance and ensuring that all of the necessary requirements of the contract are met. In some instances this may mean coordinating the interfaces among multiple vendors as well as administering each of the respective contracts.

Concluding Project Executing, Monitoring, and Controlling

With the project executing, monitoring and controlling complete your next step is to close the project. Fill in the blanks below to see how much you understood and retained from the material that was just presented.

STOP TO
COMPLETE
ACTIVITY

Applying to the Next Project

Discussion Questions

1. What is the definition of project execution? Why is project execution important?

2. What are the multiple actions required to be completed as a part of project execution?

3. What is the purpose of quality assurance? What does quality assurance entail?

4. How are team members acquired? What does this process entail?

    _____

    _____

    _____

    _____

    _____

    _____

5. What does developing the project team entail? Why it is important to develop the team? Who is responsible for project-team development?

    _____

    _____

    _____

    _____

    _____

    _____

6. Why is distributing project information important? How is it done? How does the lessons-learned activity fit into the overall process?

    _____

    _____

    _____

    _____

    _____

7. What is the purpose of monitoring and controlling the project?

    _____

    _____

    _____

    _____

    _____

8. What are the activities that take place in monitoring and controlling the project plan?

    _____

    _____

    _____

    _____

    _____

9. What is the purpose of integrated change control? What activities take place in this area?

10. What is the purpose of scope verification and scope control? What takes place in each of these areas?

11. Why is monitoring and controlling the project schedule important?

12. Why it is important to monitor and control cost in a project?

13. What is the purpose of performing quality control when monitoring and controlling the project?

14. What is the purpose of performance reporting as a part of managing and controlling the project plan?

_____

_____

_____

_____

_____

_____

15. What activities take place as a part of risk monitoring and controlling?

_____

_____

_____

_____

_____

16. What activities take place as a part of contract administration?

_____

_____

_____

_____

_____

STOP TO
COMPLETE
ACTIVITY ## Instructions

1. Use the details that you compiled in the previous activities to complete the relevant templates below.

2. Feel free to use any templates that you may already have in place in your organization as a substitute for or in addition to what is presented below.

Change Management Plan Template

Some fields include instruction on how to populate the document

Project Name:	
Prepared by:	
Date:	

1. Purpose
Ensure that all changes to the project are reviewed and approved in advance
All changes are coordinated across the entire project
All stakeholders are notified of approved changes to the project

2. Goals
Consider all requests for change
Define, evaluate, approve and track changes through to completion
Modify project plans to reflect the impact of the requested changes
Bring the appropriate parties into the discussion
Negotiate changes and communicate them to all affected parties

3. Responsibilities

Those Responsible for Change Management	Responsibilities
Project manager and project team	Developing the change management plan
Project manager	Facilitating or executing the change management process. This process may result in changes to the scope, schedule, budget, and/or quality plans. Additional resources may be needed.
Designated member of the project team	Maintain a log of all change requests
Project manager	Conducting reviews of all change management activities with senior management on a periodic basis
The executive committee	Ensuring that the change management plan is implemented and that adequate resources and funding are available to support execution of the change management plan.

4. Process (the change management process may be simple or complex. The text below is provided as an example of how requests for change may be handled on your project)

Any stakeholder may request or identify a change. He/she uses a change request form to document the nature of the change request. The change request is submitted in writing.

The completed form is sent to a designated member of the project team who enters the change request into the project change request log.

The change requests are reviewed daily by the project manager or a designee. The outcome of the decision may be to reject, defer to another date, accept for analysis immediately (in cases of emergency), or accept for consideration by the project team).

If approved, perform analysis and develop a recommendation

Accept or reject the recommendation

If accepted, update project documents revise plans

Notify all stakeholders of the change

5. Notes on the Change-control process

A change request is included in the project only when both the sponsor and the project team agree on a recommended action

The change request may be :

Low impact – No material affect on cost or schedule. Quality is not impaired.

Medium impact – Moderate impact on cost or schedule, or no impact on cost and schedule but quality is impaired. If the impact is negative, the sponsor may review and approval is required.

High impact – Significant impact on cost, schedule or quality. If impact is negative, executive committee review and approval is required.

Whenever changes are made to project documents, the version history is updated in the document and prior versions are maintained in an archive. Edit access to project documents is limited to the project manager and designated individuals on the project team.

6. Change Management Plan Signatures

I have reviewed the information contained in the change management plan and agree

Name	Role	Signature	Date

The signatures above indicate an understanding of the purpose and content of this document by those signing it. By signing this document, they agree to this as the formal project change management plan document.

Change Request Form Template

Some fields include instruction on how to populate the document

Project Name:	
Prepared by:	
Date:	

1. Requestor Information (Fill in with appropriate information or place an "X" next to those that apply)

Area of change:

Scope   [   ]   Schedule   [   ]

Budget   [   ]   Quality   [   ]

Is this change as a result of a risk-management action?

Yes   [   ]   No   [   ]

Proposed change description and reference

Description:

Justification:

Supporting Detail:

Impact of NOT Implementing Proposed Change:

Alternatives:

2. Initial Review – Results of the Change Request

Initial Review Date:

Assigned to:

Action Comments
Approve [ ]

Reject [ ]

Defer until (specify date) [ ]

Express Approval [ ]

3. Initial Impact Analysis
Baselines affected:
Impact on cost:
Impact on schedule:
Impact on resources:
Risk associated with implementing change:
Risk associated with not implementing change:
Final review results:
Review date:
Priority: (check one) High [ ] Medium [ ] Low [ ]
4. Impact Analysis Results
Specific requirements definition:
Additional resource requirements. Work days Cost:
Total:
Impact of NOT implementing the change:
Alternatives to the proposed change:
5. Final Recommendation

6. Change Request Form Signatures			
I have reviewed the information contained in the change request form and agree			
Name	Role	Signature	Date

The signatures above indicate an understanding of the purpose and content of this document by those signing it. By signing this document, they agree to this as the formal project change request form document.

Meeting Minutes Template

Some fields include instruction on how to populate the document

Project Name:	
Prepared by:	
Date:	

1. Purpose of Meeting

2. Attendance at Meeting			
Name	Department	E-mail	Telephone

3. Meeting Agenda

4. Meeting Notes, Decisions, Issues

5. Action Items

Action	Assigned to	Due Date

6. Next Meeting

Date	Time	Location	Comments

Agenda

Change Log Template

Project Name:							
Prepared by:							
Date:							
Request #	Change Description and Impact to Project	Priority (H, M, L)	Reported By	Status	Date Resolved	Resolution/ Comments

Project Issue Template

Some fields include instruction on how to populate the document

Project Name:	
Prepared by:	
Date:	

1. Issue Background (Fill in with appropriate information or place an "X" next to those that apply)

Issue Type:

Request for Information [ ] Procedural Problem [ ] System Problem [ ] Other [ ]

Issue Description:

Potential Impact (if not resolved):

Attachments (if any)

Yes [ ] No [ ]

Date Resolution Needed:

2. Analysis

Reviewer Name:

Review Completion Date:

Reviewer Comments:

Initial Recommendation:

Cost/Schedule Impact Analysis Required? Yes [ ] No [ ]

Proposed Assignee:

Estimate of Additional Effort: (insert rows as needed)

Resources Required	Work Days/Costs

3. Recommendation (final recommendation and comments)

Name	Title	Signature	Date

4. Management Action

Recommendation Status: Fill in with appropriate information or place an X next to those that apply

Accept [ ] Defer [ ] Reject [ ] Need Additional Information [ ]

Assigned to:

Planned Completion Date:

Name	Title	Date	Comment

5. Project Issue Document Signatures

I have reviewed the information contained in the project issue document and agree

Name	Role	Signature	Date

The signatures above indicate an understanding of the purpose and content of this document by those signing it. By signing this document, they agree to this as the formal project issue document.

Project Issue Template

Project Name:	
Prepared by:	
Date:	

Request #	Issue Description and Impact to Project	Priority (H, M, L)	Reported By	Status	Date Resolved	Resolution/ Comments

Project Monthly Status Report Template

Some fields include instruction on how to populate the document

Project Name:	
Prepared by:	
Date:	

1. Executive Summary

Overall Status:

	1. Green (Controlled	2. Yellow (Caution)	3. Red (Critical)	Reason for Deviation
Budget:				
Schedule:				
Scope:				
Quality				

1 = Project is within budget, scope and on schedule
2 = Project has deviated slightly from the plan but should recover
3 = Project has fallen significantly behind schedule, is forecasted to be significantly over budget, and/or has taken on tasks that are out of scope.

Comments

2. Controls

Issue Status (issues requiring resolution by project team or executive committee)

Change Status (changes raised for consideration that change the approved project baselines. Would require approval by the project sponsor and possibly the executive committee)

Risk Status (report on any changes in priority or status of major project risks, and any risks discovered since earlier risk assessments along with proposed risk response)

3. Budget Report

Expense	Budget to Date	Actual to Date	Variance	Estimate to Complete	Budget Total Cost	Estimate at Completion

Comments

4. Scheduled Milestones/Deliverables

List any project milestones that are late as well as milestones due in the next 4 – 6 weeks.

Milestone	Approved Schedule	Actual	Current Forecast	Status

5. Accomplishments/Plans

Accomplishments during this reporting period (should relate to milestones)

Plans during the next reporting period (should relate to milestones)

6. Monthly Status Report Signatures

I have reviewed the information contained in the monthly status report and agree

Name	Role	Signature	Date

The signatures above indicate an understanding of the purpose and content of this document by those signing it. By signing this document, they agree to this as the project monthly status report document.

THE FOUR-STEP COMBO

Step 4

Chapter 8
Evaluation and Closing the Project

After studying this chapter, you should be able to

- state the level and the associated measurement category in the Phillips ROI Evaluation Model.

- define formative evaluation and give examples of formative evaluation measures in the automated sales-management system training program.

- define summative evaluation and give examples of summative evaluation measures in the automated sales-management system training program.

- describe the project-closeout process.

- list the three reasons why projects end.

- describe the four types of project endings.

- list some things that must take place in project closing.

As you read this chapter, be sure that you understand the following terms and ideas.

- Phillips ROI Model
- Project Closeout
- Starvation
- Formative Evaluation
- Integration
- Summative Evaluation
- Addition
- Extinction

You initiate your out-of-office message to inform readers that you are away from the office on holiday for two weeks with no access to e-mails. All messages are referred to the boss until your return.

You shut down your personal computer, pack up your desk, and you're officially on holiday. A well-deserved holiday, at that. The project is over, evaluations are in, project closure documents in place. By all accounts, the initiative is a success. But that's not without mental and physical toll on you. But who cares, it's over now and you're out of office.

Overview

It's been a long journey from idea conception, project initiation, planning, executing, monitoring and controlling. The four-step combo concludes with a review of evaluation (formative and summative) and project closeout. Two project-management processes are included in the closing-process group. These include close project and contract closure. All processes should be considered, although not necessarily performed as a part of the project-closing process. The decision on the processes to be performed is based on the size and complexity of the project.

Evaluation

Phillips ROI Evaluation Model

The Phillips ROI Model differentiates the levels of evaluation as follows:

Level 1   Reaction and Planned Action – Measures learners' reaction to the program and outlines specific plans for implementation

Level 2   Learning – Measures skills, knowledge, or change in attitude

Level 3   Application and Implementation – Measures changes in behavior on the job through specific application

Level 4   Business Impact – Measures business impact of the program

Level 5   Return on Investment – Compares the monetary value of the results of the program to the cost

Formative Evaluation

Formative evaluation takes place before the learning program is actually delivered. In the case of the automated sales-management system training program, formative evaluation included usability testing in addition to validating the training program.

In usability testing, a sample of end users actually used the prototype while being observed by the instructional designer. Reactions were recorded and appropriate revisions were made.

Benefits of Formative Evaluation

Benefits associated with formative evaluation include the following.

- Difficulties are detected and remedied before full production.

- Instructional designers become more sensitive to user needs and become better at designing user-friendly products.

Summative Evaluations

Evaluations that take place during and after delivery of the training program are considered summative evaluations. They provide evidence to sponsors and potential users about the value of the learning solution.

It is important that evaluation is built into the training program from the foundation. In the case of the automated sales-management-systems training, an evaluation strategy was incorporated into the needs analysis and the learning strategy.

The instructional designer uses various methods to ensure that evaluation measures are obtained at various stages in the learning program. Using different methods to evaluate activities and outputs provides quality assurance throughout the process.

Criteria and methods are used to measure learning during the course delivery. In the case of the automated sales-management training, additional evaluation methods are used to measure the application of knowledge and skill on the job. Methods for gathering on the job data include the following.

- On-the-job observation

- Interviews and/or questionnaires completed by learners and their supervisors and managers

- Check up on action plans made during training

Most importantly, summative evaluation must link back to business impact measures.

Non-Training Support

Instructional designers should work with managers and supervisors of the learners to ensure that the appropriate workplace changes necessary to support trainee transfer of knowledge and skill on the job is in place. This involves non-training interventions such as supervisor observation and support as well as reward and recognition of the use of new knowledge and skill.

Project Closeout

During the closing processes (close project and contract closure), the project acceptance is documented with a formal sign-off. These documents are filed with the project records for future reference.

While the automated sales-management system ended successfully, it is important to know that projects come to an end for some of the reasons presented below.

- They are successfully completed.

- They are canceled or killed prior to completion.

- They evolve into ongoing operations and no longer exist as projects.

Four Types of Project Endings

The four formal types of project endings (addition, starvation, integration, and extinction) are outlined as follows:

Addition
This is a term that is used to describe projects that evolve into ongoing operations; in other words, they become their own ongoing business unit.

Starvation
A project is starved when resources are cut off from the project or are no longer provided to the project. Starvation can happen for some of the reasons outlined as follows.

- Other projects come about and take precedence over the current project, thereby cutting the funding or resources.

- The customer curtails the order.

- The project budget is reduced.

- A key resource leaves the organization.

Integration
Integration occurs when the project resources (people, equipment, supplies) are distributed to other areas of the organization or are assigned to other projects.

Extinction

Extinction means that the project is complete.

The key activity in closing out the project is concerned with gathering project records and disseminating information to formalize the acceptance of the product, service, or project. Once the project outcomes are documented, the project manager requests formal acceptance from stakeholders or the customer.

The closeout procedure also includes analyzing the project-management processes to determine their effectiveness and to document lessons learned concerning the project processes. All project documents are then archived for historical reference.

Close Project

Closing the project requires that you begin with accepted deliverables, the project-management plan, and/organizational-process assets, all of which are discussed below.

- *Accepted Deliverables*

    Accepted deliverables are defined as those deliverables for which approval and final sign-off is obtained by the customer or sponsor.

- *Project-Management Plan*

    The project-management plan contains the subsidiary management plans and baselines from the planning process. The project-management plan includes information and instructions on how various processes will be applied, how work will be accepted and how changes will be addressed throughout the project duration.

- *Organizational-Process Assets*

    Project-closure guidelines or requirements (e.g., project audits, project evaluations and transition criteria), historical information, and lessons learned are examples of organizational-process assets that are addressed during the project-closure process.

The Method

- *Expert Judgment*

    Expert judgment is the only method used to ensure that project closure is performed at the appropriate standard.

The Result

- *Final Product, Service or Result Transition*

  The final product, service, or result that the project was authorized to produce is transitioned to operations or to the next phase as a part of project closure.

- *Organizational-Process Assets Updates*

  The project-management plan, scope, cost, schedule and project calendars, risk registers, change management documentation, planned risk response actions and risk impact, are formal documentation indicating completion of the project or phase and the transfer of deliverables to operations or the next phase. Relevant contracts and historical information such as lessons learned are examples of organizational-process assets that require update as a part of project closure.

Close Procurements

Closing procurements requires that you begin with procurement documentation and the project-management plan, both of which are discussed below.

- *Procurement Documentation*

  All information on contract schedule, scope, quality, and cost performance along with contract-change documentation, payment records, inspection results, and all procurement documentation is collected, indexed, and filed as a part of contract closure.

- *Project-Management Plan*

  The project-management plan contains the subsidiary management plans and baselines from the planning process. The project-management plan includes information and instructions on how various processes will be applied, how work will be accepted and how changes will be addressed throughout the project duration.

The Method

The three methods used when closing procurements are presented below.

- *Procurement Audits*

  The procurement audit is a structured review of the procurement process that is intended to identify successes and failure as it relates to the preparation or administration of procurement contracts that relate to the project.

• *Negotiated Settlements*

It is necessary to finalize all negotiated settlements of outstanding claims, issues, and disputes as they relate to procurement.

• *Records-Management System*

Records-management system involves policies, control functions and automated tools as a part of the project-management information system. Records-management systems provide a means of indexing documents for easy filing and retrieval.

The Result

• *Closed Procurements*

The buyer is expected to provide the seller with formal written notice that the contract is complete according to the agreed-upon terms in the contract.

• *Organizational-Process Assets Updates*

A complete set of indexed documentations including closed contract, formal written notice from the buyer that the deliverables are accepted or rejected, and lessons learned are examples of organizational-process assets that are a part of close procurements.

STOP TO COMPLETE ACTIVITY	**Applying to the Next Project**
	Discussion Questions

1. What is the definition of the project-closeout process?

   _____

   _____

   _____

   _____

   _____

   _____

2. What are the three reasons why projects end?

   _____

   _____

_____
_____
_____
_____

3. What are the four types of project endings?

_____
_____
_____
_____
_____
_____

4. What are some things that must take place in project closing?

_____
_____
_____
_____
_____

| STOP TO COMPLETE ACTIVITY | **Instructions** |

1. Use the details that you compiled in the previous activities to complete the template below.

2. Feel free to use any templates that you may already have in place in your organization as a substitute for or in addition to what is presented below.

Project Lessons-Learned Checklist

Project Name:	
Prepared By:	
Date	

Use this lessons-learned checklist as an aid to understanding those factors that either helped or hindered the project.

- Best used in a group discussion among those who have a stake in the project
- May be used at anytime as a discussion tool, or may be used during project close as a part of the lessons-learned exercise

1. Project Lessons-Learned Checklist									
Instructions: **Yes** = The project team agrees with the statement. **No** = The project team does not agree with the statement. **N/A** = This statement does not apply to the project. **Impact** = The extent to which this factor had an impact on your project.									
No.		Yes	No	N/A	Impact				
					Low			High	
					1	2	3	4	5
1.	Business objectives were specific, measurable, attainable, results focused, and time limited.								
2.	Product concept was appropriate to business objectives.								
3.	Project plan and schedule were well documented with appropriate structure and detail.								
4.	Project schedule encompassed all aspects of the project.								
5.	Tasks were adequately defined.								
6.	Stakeholders (e.g., sponsor, customer) had appropriate input into the project-planning process.								
7.	Requirements were gathered to sufficient detail.								
8.	Requirements were documented clearly.								
9.	Specifications were clear and well documented.								
10.	Design documents were adequate, understandable, and well documented.								
11.	External dependencies were identified and agreements signed.								
12.	Project budget was well defined.								

13.	End-of-phase criteria were clear for all project phases.								

1. Project Lessons-Learned Checklist Cont.

Instructions:

Yes = The project team agrees with the statement.
No = The project team does not agree with the statement.
N/A = This statement does not apply to the project.
Impact = The extent to which this factor had an impact on your project

No.		Yes	No	N/A	Impact				
					Low			High	
					1	2	3	4	5
14.	Project plan had buy-in from all stakeholders.								
15.	Stakeholders had easy access to project plan and schedule.								
	Project Execution and Delivery								
16.	Project stuck to its original goals.								
17.	Changes in direction that did occur were of manageable frequency and magnitude.								
18.	Project baselines (scope, time, cost, and quality) were well managed (e.g., changed through a formal change-control process).								
19.	Design changes were well controlled.								
20.	Basic project-management processes (e.g., risk management, issue management) were adequate.								
21.	Project tracked progress against baselines and reported accurate status.								
22.	Procurement process went smoothly.								
23.	Contracted vendor provided acceptable deliverables of appropriate quality, on time, and within budget.								
24.	Stakeholders were satisfied with the information that they received.								
25.	The project had adequate quality control.								
26.	Risks were managed.								
	Human Factors								
27.	Project manager was effective.								
28.	Project team was properly organized and staffed.								
29.	Project team's talent and experience were adequate.								
30.	Project team worked effectively on project goals.								
31.	Project team worked effectively with outside entities.								

No.	1. Project Lessons Learned Checklist Cont.	Yes	No	N/A	Impact				
	Instructions: **Yes** = The project team agrees with the statement. **No** = The project team does not agree with the statement. **N/A** = This statement does not apply to the project. **Impact** = The extent to which this factor had an impact on your project.				Low		High		
					1	2	3	4	5
32.	There was good communication within the project team.								
33.	Management gave this project adequate attention and time.								
34.	Resources were not over-committed.								
35.	Resources were consistently committed to project teams.								
36.	Functional areas cooperated well.								
37.	Conflicting department goals did not cause problems.								
38.	Authority and accountability were well defined and public.								
	Overall								
39.	Initial cost and schedule estimates were accurate.								
40.	Product was delivered within amended schedule.								
41.	Product was delivered within amended budget.								
42.	Overall change control was effective.								
43.	External dependencies were understood and well managed.								
44.	Technology chosen was appropriate.								
45.	Customer's needs/requirements were met.								
46.	Customer was satisfied with the product.								
47.	Product objectives were met.								
48.	Business objectives were met.								

2. Project Lessons-Learned Checklist – Agreement Form/Signatures

Project Name:	
Project Manager:	

I have reviewed the information contained in this Project Lessons-Learned Checklist and agree:

Name	Title	Signature	Date

The signatures above indicate an understanding of the purpose and content of this document by those signing it. By signing this document, all parties agree to this as the formal project lessons-learned checklist.

Summary

Grooving to the Beat of the Four-Step Combo

Congratulations; you are successfully at the end of the project. You should be grooving to the beat of the four-step combo. Let's recap.

Recall that the mandate to design, develop, and deliver an automated sales-management training program for sales officers began with a conversation between the boss and the instructional designer. After defining a project and identifying respective stakeholder groups, it was determined that the situation presented by the boss fit the definition of a project. The decision was made to combine two disciplines, instructional-systems development and project management, based on the Project Management Institute and the PMBOK best practices. These disciplines were blended in a way that was fluid, interconnected, and sequential to the way that an instructional designer may work. Once ADDIE and project management were united, the four-step combo was born.

Step 1 of the Four-Step Combo

Analysis

The instructional-systems design model was introduced with an overview and a discussion of what to consider when conducting an analysis. A comparative analysis between actual and expected business and performance results was presented in the form of a needs-analysis document. The findings of the needs analysis revealed gaps in knowledge and skill and the decision was made to design, develop and deliver a learning solution to close the identified gaps.

Initiating the Project Plan

A review of project initiation was presented. The presentation method included the following:
- Definition of project initiation
- Essential ingredients necessary for initiating a project
- Method that should be used for initiating a project
- Result of initiating a project

Sample documents produced as a result of project initiation were introduced for review.

Step 2 of the Four-Step Combo

Creating the Design Document

The design document was introduced in step two of the four-step combo and included a description of how the information from the needs analysis is typically communicated. A sample of a design document populated with information was included for review.

Creating the Project-Management Plan

A review of the project-planning process was introduced. The presentation method included the following:

- Definition of the project plan and subsidiary plans
- Essential ingredients necessary to develop the project plan and subsidiary documents
- Methods that should be used for developing the project plan and subsidiary documents
- Results of the project plan and subsidiary documents

Sample subsidiary documents were populated with information and presented for review.

Step 3 of the Four-Step Combo

Developing and Implementing the Product

The design document progressed to development. Information on the communication process was introduced. Such information included barriers to effective communication, creating positive expectations, projecting credibility, creating a climate, previewing the content, and fitting the message together. Material on validating the course material was also made available to the reader.

Executing and Monitoring and Controlling the Project Plan

Project execution and monitoring and controlling was introduced in the third step of the four-step combo. The presentation method included the following:

- Definition of the project executing and monitoring and controlling subsidiary plans
- Essential ingredients necessary for project execution and monitoring and controlling the project plan and subsidiary documents
- Methods that should be used for executing and monitoring and controlling the project plan and subsidiary documents
- Results of project executing and monitoring and controlling the project plan and subsidiary documents

Step 4 of the Four-Step Combo

Evaluating and Closing the Project

The four-step combo concluded with a review of evaluation (formative and summative) and project close out.

Chapter 9

Cases in Project Management for the Instructional Designer

A Guide to Case Analysis

Objectives of Case Analysis

Using cases to learn about how the disciplines of project management and instructional design are used is a powerful way to accomplish the following things:

- Increase your understanding of what the instructional designer should and should not do in the context of managing the design, development, delivery, and evaluation of learning solutions.

- Get valuable practice with analyzing, initiating, designing, planning, developing, implementing, executing, monitoring, controlling, evaluating, and closing projects.

- Enhance your sense of business judgment.

Case discussions are often not intended to produce concrete answers. Instead, case discussions usually produce good arguments for more than one course of action. There are often several feasible courses of action and approaches that may be used in any given scenario. The objective of case analysis is to think actively, offer analysis, propose action plans, and explain and defend the assessment.

204 ► Dorcas M. T. Cox

Preparing for Case Discussion

The following approach may be used when preparing for case discussions:

1. **Read the Case**

   Reading over the case introduces you to the situation and the issue(s) involved.

2. **Decide on the Issues**

   Identify the strategic issues and problems in the case to determine what to analyze, what are the essential inputs, which tool and techniques are required, and what are the expected outputs. At times, the strategic issues are clear. At other times, you may have to dig the information out from the information that is presented.

3. **Use the Necessary Inputs, Tools and Techniques, and Outputs**

   Effective project management based on the framework and standards of the Project Management Institute and the PMBOK Guide best practices is not merely a collection of opinions; rather, it entails application of a significant number of inputs, tools and techniques, and outputs to respective knowledge areas and process groups.

   Applying the proper knowledge of project-management methodology in this way cuts beneath the surface and produces important insight and understanding of strategic situations.

4. **Consider Conflicting Opinions**

   Contradictory opinions and views often surface during case discussions. This forces the analyst to develop skill in inference and judgment. A great many managerial situations entail opposing points of view, conflicting trends, and sketchy information.

5. **Support Your Diagnosis and Opinions with Reasons and Evidence**

   It is important that the analyst prepare for the question "Why?" For example, if after reviewing the case, you are of the opinion that the project manager or the functional manager should act in a certain way, prepare to support your diagnosis and opinions with reasons and evidence.

6. **Develop an Appropriate Plan and Set of Recommendations**

   It is important to convert sound analysis into sound actions that are intended to produce the desired results. The final and most telling step in preparing a case is to develop an action agenda for management that lays out a set of specific recommendations on what to do. The analyst should be prepared to argue why their recommendations are more attractive than other courses of action that may be open.

Participating in Class Discussions

The following is a list of things to expect in the classroom discussion environment.

- Expect that learners will dominate the discussion and do most of the talking. The case method requires maximum individual participation in class discussion. Being present as a silent observer throughout the entire period of time allocated for class discussion will not realize the desired result for the learner or their peers.

- Expect the instructor/facilitator to assume the role of extensive questioner and objective listener.

- Be prepared for the instructor/facilitator to probe for reasons and supporting detail based on analysis.

- Expect challenges and opposing views to those expressed as learners submit their conclusions for scrutiny and rebuttal. Learning to respect the views and approaches of others is integral to case analysis exercises.

- Remember that it is alright to change your mind about your initial views, assumptions, and conclusions as the discussion unfolds.

- Expect to learn a lot from each case discussion. Use what you learn to be better prepared for the next case discussion and on-the-job application.

Additional Tips for Case Discussions

The following is a list of tips that may be used during case discussions:

- Do not hesitate to discuss the case before and after class with your peers. Developing effective communication skills is critical to the success of the instructional designer and the project manager. Managers often discuss their case scenarios with others to refine their own thinking.

- Make a conscious effort to participate in case discussions rather than merely talking. Ensure that your comments add value to and build the discussion.

- Always prepare good notes for each case and refer to your notes if necessary during your presentation.

Preparing a Written Case Analysis

There is no standard procedure for preparing a written case analysis; at the same time, there are some general guidelines that may be useful. These guidelines are presented in three steps: identification, analysis, and evaluation and recommendations.

Step 1 – Identification

Provide a sharply focused diagnosis of strategic issues and key problems early on in your paper. Demonstrate a clear understanding of the company's present state. Make sure that you can identify the strategy and articulate whatever strategy implementation issues may exist.

Begin your discussion with a summary of the company's situation, its strategy, and the significant problems and issues that confront management. State problems and/or issues as precisely as you can.

Step 2 – Analysis and Evaluation

Determine if the company's strategy is producing satisfactory results and determine the reasons why or why not. Determine the need for and/or results of a needs analysis. Determine the need for project initiation. State the tasks in the respective knowledge areas and process groups in addition to the respective inputs, outputs, tools, and techniques that will be used from project initiation to closure.

Introduce evidence to support your conclusions. Do not rely on overgeneralizations or unsupported opinion. Use tables and/or charts to present the quantitative analysis. Demonstrate the use of the concepts and analytical tools incorporated in the instructional design and project-management discipline.

Make sure that the interpretation of the data in the case study is reasonable and objective. Be careful to present a balanced argument.

Step 3 – Recommendations

The final section of the written case analysis should consist of a set of definite recommendations, along with an action plan. Recommendations should address all of the problems/issues identified and analyzed. Check to see if your recommendations are workable in terms of acceptance by the persons involved and the organization's ability to implement them.

Case 1
PJ Enterprises

PJ Enterprises is a mail-order catalog business that has been in operation for the past six years. The company develops, manufactures, and markets high-quality gifts, apparel, and home accessories and distributes them through its mail-order catalog and its retail store. The company focuses on the needs of women between the ages of twenty-five and fifty-five years who own their own homes and have family incomes between $40,000 and $80,000. PJ Enterprises believes that female catalog shoppers look for traditional, nostalgic, and romantic gifts, apparel, and home accessories to enhance the quality of their homes and family lives.

PJ Enterprises catalog offerings include sweaters, skirts, and novelty items. Unique jewelry such as pins, earrings, belts, necklaces, and bracelets are also included in the catalog. Children's products including puzzles and toys for children ages two to ten years as well as lamps, rugs, and other accessories to bring traditional or nostalgic appearance to children's rooms are also found in the catalog. The catalog also includes evergreen wreaths, centerpieces, collectable handcraft figurines, plates, dolls, and other inspirational and symbolic items reflecting traditional values.

At present, the catalog division of PJ Enterprises is located in a building that has four thousand feet of office space and six thousand square feet of warehouse space. At present, the company pays about $5,000 per month in principal and interest for the use of the space.

PJ Enterprises recorded a profit for this year with annual sales of $6 million dollars. Despite the recession, high points for this year included the following:

- Thirty-one percent increase in catalog customer lists to 250,000 names
- Forty-one percent increase in sales
- Net profit of $1 million for this fiscal year

Business Plan Goals

The management team of PJ Enterprises is presently negotiating the business plan for the upcoming year. Some concerns expressed include whether it is reasonable to expect that the company will continue to grow at the present rate. If so, could the present management team facilitate and control the growth while remaining profitable? Where should the company grow? How will this be achieved? What financial, human resources, and other resources would be required?

Last Year's Targets	This Year's Targets
$5 million in annual sales	$7 million in annual sales
$10 million in catalog sales	$13 million in catalog sales
$5 million from the retail division	$7 million from the retail division
$10 million from acquisitions	$12 million from acquisitions
21% increase in customer lists	40% increase in customer lists
Net profit of $1 million	Net profit of $2 million

Business Objectives

- Aggressive growth to maintain or exceed projected targets
- Maintain profitability
- Focus on quality and customer service with 10 percent improvement on customer-service scores
- Focus on quality of work environment and staff development and recognition

The company estimates capital expenditures of $400,000 to $500,000 would be needed to increase catalog sales to the $13 million dollar mark. There is also a need to increase the company's customer list. The larger the house list, the less need for the company to rent other lists. As the house list grows, promotional costs decrease as net sales increase. The company can also earn money from the rental of its own house list.

Organization and Staffing

PJ Enterprises' catalog division presently employs fifty people. Forty staff are employed on a full-time basis. Included in the number of employees are four customer-service supervisors and twenty-five telephone operators.

The catalog director, Judie Thompson, is responsible for all aspects of the catalogs. This year is the first year that the company produced four different catalogs—one for each season. Previously, the summer catalog was essentially the spring catalog with sale prices. The spring catalog, featuring Easter gift items, was forty pages and was mailed in the end of December. The summer catalog was thirty-two pages and was mailed in mid-April. The forty-page fall catalog featured Halloween, Thanksgiving, and some Christmas items and was mailed in the end of June. The biggest-ever Christmas catalog was forty-eight pages and was mailed in mid-September.

Sheena Perez, the merchandising manager, is responsible for selecting and promoting items for the catalogs. Sheena and Judie frequent gift, apparel, and other trade shows throughout the year, seeking vendors with quality products and reputation for reliability in shipping. They bring potential catalog items back to the office where they, along with the assistant merchandising manager, examine each piece and argue for or against offering it to the PJ Enterprises catalog customers.

After the catalog merchandise is selected, Sheena Perez works closely with a contract copywriter and professional service firms contracted to design and produce the catalog including layout, photography, and printing. The vendor selection process includes interviewing, negotiating, inspecting, and managing. Before the catalogs are mailed, the customer-service supervisors and the telephone operators are trained on each catalog item. This training is conducted by Sheena Perez, the merchandising manager, and Judie Thompson, the catalog director.

This half-day training is conducted using a PowerPoint presentation method. Thirty minutes are reserved at the end of the meeting for questions and answers. Training materials include a summary product description for easy reference on the automated entry system. Product catalog training is conducted four times per year prior to the introduction of the new season's catalog.

At present, the company has rotated more than five hundred products through its catalogs over the six years that it has been in operation.

Quality and Service

PJ Enterprises has a goal of quality service delivery. The company has a toll-free telephone number for placing orders and for customer-service inquiries and complaints. Its present telephone system can support twenty incoming lines and forty headsets and has automatic call-distribution features and activity-reporting capability. The results of a brief customer-service survey that the telephone operators are required to conduct with every customer are also captured as a part of the activity reporting. Telephone operators can access product reference guides and answer questions while the customer is on the line.

The phone lines are staffed twenty-four hours per day, seven days per week. The telephone operator answers telephone calls using the standard greeting, places the order directly on the system, and encourages the customer to answer a few brief customer-service questions. If the customer requires service, the telephone operator transfers the call to the customer service supervisor on duty. The present system is designed to answer 90 percent of all customer inquiries within two minutes and to ensure that the customer is kept happy. At the moment, the telephone system is only used at 85 percent capacity.

Reports generated by the system indicate that each telephone operator only responds to three calls per hour as opposed to the required number of six calls per hour. Customer-service data reveal that two customers out of every three who respond to the customer-service survey have a complaint about the telephone operator. Complaints are typically around product knowledge, telephone etiquette, and prompt response to calls waiting in the queue. Customers complain that even after the long wait to speak to a telephone operator, they are asked to call back or are redirected to a customer service supervisor to have their query answered satisfactorily. Fifty percent of the customers surveyed from last year responded that they are not inclined to do business with PJ Enterprises again as a result of the poor customer service that they received.

The average order is between $250–$500 dollars, so revenue is generated by call volume and sales volume. Customer benefits include competitive prices, optional overnight delivery, and quick shipping from receipt of order.

PJ Enterprises stresses the importance of quality in all aspects of the work, from producing the catalog to taking, packing, and shipping an order. Incentives are awarded for both warehouse and customer-service staff for error-free performance.

Issues for Management

- Upgrade of current hardware configuration with additional work stations as well as new equipment and technical improvement in the warehouse is necessary for the projected increase in catalog sales.

- Human resources challenges continue to be a concern for the company's management team. One of the greatest challenges is recruiting, selection, hiring, training, and managing new people. There is a high turnover of staff on all levels, particularly with the telephone operators, customer-service supervisors, and warehouse staff. On average, one staff member resigns or is terminated every other month.

- Just recently, some new HR policies were introduced to the staff. These policies include a performance evaluation/self-evaluation process, a new company handbook, and an upgrade to the company's pension plan.

- Employee meetings are now scheduled to be held once per month but often times are very poorly attended because of the employees' working hours. Employees are not compensated for attending these meetings.

- Customer-survey figures indicate an increase of 30 percent in customer complaints with the telephone operators as compared to the same period last year.

- More than half of the total number of telephone operators were informally interviewed and indicated dissatisfaction with their jobs to the point of leaving.

Practical Exercise

In light of the aggressive targets and alleged employee dissatisfaction among telephone operators in particular, senior management is proposing the use of a slightly different approach for the training that is typically conducted before the catalog mailing.

As the instructional designer and project manager, you are hired by PJ Enterprises to design, develop, and deliver a learning program for the telephone operators. The training course is intended to be delivered before the catalogs are mailed.

The target audience is customer-service supervisors and the telephone operators. Participants are to be trained on each catalog item. The course that you will design, develop, and deliver will substitute the training course that was previously conducted by Sheena Perez, the merchandising manager, and Judie Thompson, the catalog director.

Management believes that increase in knowledge and skill in describing the features and benefits of the products in the catalog is necessary to increase catalog sales and reduce customer complaints.

A budget of $400,000 is allocated for all staff training during the upcoming fiscal year.

Review the details in the case presented above and consider how you may use your knowledge and skill in instructional design and project management to address the situation above.

Use the data provided in the case to complete all project management and/or instructional design documents that you recommend to be completed as a part of this case analysis. Submit these documents, along with your written case findings, for grading.

Case 2
Liz and Jim Takeout

Liz and Jim Takeout has been in operation for the past three years. The menu features fried chicken, fried fish, fried pork chops, hot dogs, hamburgers, french fries, and fountain sodas. Liz and Jim McKenzie started the business with little more than their life savings and a dream of success. Neither of them had extensive background in business nor restaurant operations.

The initial investment was approximately $315,000. The majority of the funds was for land and a building, which totaled $200,000. The equipment investment was about $85,000, and working-capital requirements were about $30,000.

Liz and Jim's first order of business was to hire a professional in kitchen design who created a unique kitchen layout designed for fast and efficient service. The kitchen layout is very efficient in everything from storage, inventory control, and cooking efficiency to order delivery.

Liz and Jim's business strategy was to do everything as simply as possible and avoid sophisticated accounting systems and legal agreements. As Liz and Jim's Takeout grew in popularity, so did the number of persons on staff. Head count swelled from three persons in the first year of business to thirty persons. The rapid expansion seemed to be getting out of hand. Liz and Jim wasted no time in hiring persons for the store, most of whom were members of their direct or extended family. In recent months, quarrelling has begun among some family members. This has impacted sales, service, and overall staff morale.

Jim McKenzie has always been a reluctant leader who despises conflict and often feels uncomfortable in any kind of meeting, even if the audience is only a few friends. Although generally well liked by most people in the organization, Jim faces a major crisis in the business that he and his wife started with little more than their life savings and a dream of success. With sales, profits, and service continuing to decline, Jim McKenzie convinces his wife Liz to agree to go outside of the company and bring in a professional manager who has no ties to the direct or extended family. In Jim McKenzie's view, housecleaning is in order and special management talent is needed.

Six months ago, Bradshaw Hamilton, a professional manager, was brought in to turn the company around. Bradshaw's initial assessment of the company revealed the following.

- The company was not making any money.

- No management strategies, goals, or plans were in place.

- The company's image was old and faded.

- The company was not advertising.

- The company was not training its employees.

- No money was being reinvested into the company.

- There was no formal system of communication in place.

Customers

For the first time in the company's history, market research was conducted. Results from the research are presented as follows:

- Typical customers are females between the ages of eighteen to twenty-four years old.

- The annual income of customers is $10,000–$15,000.

- The typical customer is a blue-collar worker and a member of a three- or four-person household.

- Sixty percent of Liz and Jim's business was done during lunchtime.

- Thirty percent of Liz and Jim's business was done during supper time.

- Ten percent of Liz and Jim's business was conducted during other periods.

- The average cost of a meal (excluding drink) was $4.50, compared to the industry average of $5.00 for fast food.

Training

Training in food preparation and service delivery is typically done informally and on the job by the cook. The recommendation is that formal operating manuals be designed and developed covering storage, preparation of menu items, order taking, cleaning, maintaining equipment, and customer service.

Constraints for the Instructional Designer

- As the instructional designer and project manager, your functional manager assigns you the task to design and develop training operating manuals for Liz and Jim Takeout.

- You work in a balanced-matrix organization that has a project-management methodology in place that does not adhere to the framework and standards of the Project Management Institute and the PMBOK Guide best practices. The organizational structure at Liz and Jim Takeout is described as functional. There is no project-management methodology in place and no appreciation for what project management is all about.

- Bradshaw Hamilton successfully completed a course in project management as a part of his MBA program a few years ago; as such, Bradshaw is familiar with the discipline. At the same time, Bradshaw also realizes that time is of the essence. Jim McKenzie needs to see results, and he needs to see results quickly. Bradshaw is on the cusp of completing his six months' probation and he does not want anything to jeopardize his formal acceptance into the organization, given that he was out of work prior to being hired by Jim McKenzie.

- Your company is commissioned by Bradshaw to do the instructional design work. Your boss has assigned the project to you. No needs analysis is necessary in this case, as the training is new.

- Bradshaw met with your boss and informed her that Liz and Jim are no-frills people who need to see results fast and do not want to get bogged down in much paper. As such, it is expected that you would not write a project charter, scope statement, or design document. The client wants you to get right to developing the course material.

- Your boss agreed to taking the work under the conditions stated by Bradshaw, as your boss needs to meet her targets for new business brought into the company for the fiscal year. Her incentive pay depends on it. Your boss assigns the project to you and conveys Bradshaw's requirements.

- Your boss has agreed that all training materials will be designed, developed, and ready for delivery within a two-month period. You have not seen the procurement documents and other vendor agreements and contracts between your company and Liz and Jim Takeaway.

Important Information for the Instructional Designer

- The cook would deliver the aspect of the course that relates to the kitchen, and the instructional designer would deliver the aspect of the course that relates to customer service.

- Your company accepts a Gantt Chart format as a project plan. Your boss does not see the necessity in producing subsidiary plans as a part of a project plan.

- Your company's policy is that your boss speaks directly to the client, Bradshaw Hamilton, and Bradshaw speaks directly to Jim McKenzie. You will never speak with Bradshaw, much less Mr. Jim McKenzie (who you may recall is averse to speaking with people whom he does not know).

Practical Exercise

Review the details of the case presented above and consider how you may use your knowledge and skill in instructional design and project management to address the situation above.

Use the data provided in the case to complete all project management and/or instructional design documents that you recommend to be completed as a part of this case analysis. Submit these documents, along with your written case findings, for grading.

Case 3
The International Company

You are an instructional designer employed by a large, multimillion-dollar organization with divisions in fifty-five countries in Latin America and the Caribbean. You work in a training department at the company's headquarters along with a team of seven instructional design managers. The team of instructional designers is managed by a senior manager of training.

The senior manager has been employed with the organization for twenty-five consecutive years, the last seven of which were in charge of the department to which you are assigned. The senior manager has spent all of her work life in the area of training. The senior manager of training has been responsible for many improvements in the department since heading the training team in the company's headquarters. Some achievements are

- the implementation of more than thirty different e-learning modules on a variety of products and services that the company provides. These modules are used by employees in the various English- and Spanish-speaking countries where the company does business.

- the implementation of the ADDIE model as the quality standard for instructional designers in the department as well as for use by training managers in the various English- and Spanish-speaking countries where the company does business.

- the introduction of a learning-management system for use within the region.

- the implementation of a number of self-study learning programs on a variety of the company's products for use within the region.

You are assigned the task by the senior manager to design and develop two self-study learning programs to meet the company's strategic objectives that were signed-off on in the strategic plan and business plan documents. Outlined below is some important information about the present state in the department that you should be aware of.

Present State in the Department

- The company has a balanced-matrix organizational structure in place.

- There is a project-management methodology in place that does not adhere to the framework and standards of the Project Management Institute and the PMBOK Guide best practices.

- Both learning programs are expected to be completed in a three-month period.

- No work-breakdown structure exists from previous projects, as completion of this task was not required by the senior manager.

- Your company accepts a Gantt Chart format as a project plan. Your boss does not see the necessity in producing subsidiary plans as a part of a project plan.

- It is not necessary for a needs analysis to be completed in this instance, as the training is new.

- Subject matter experts from various departments in headquarters as well as throughout the region will comprise an extended project team. These persons will serve as resources for you as you progress through the project from initiation to closure.

- No formal integrated change control structure exists from previous projects, as completion of this task was not required by the senior manager.

- No procurement process or vendor agreements will be used for this project.

Practical Exercise

Review the details of the case presented above and consider how you may use your knowledge and skill in instructional design and project management to address the situation above.

Use the data provided in the case to complete all project management and/or instructional design documents that you recommend to be completed as a part of this case analysis. Submit these documents, along with your written case findings, for grading.

About The Author

Dorcas Cox is the President and CEO of Project Management Solutions Ltd, a privately owned company committed to providing quality project management training and consulting solutions based on the project management body of knowledge. The company's products and services are designed to improve organizational, group, and individual performance. Dorcas has over fourteen years' consecutive experience in human resources management, instructional design, and project management. She has worked for government and multinational companies, a college/university, as a consultant, and has studied, lived, and worked in North America and Canada. Additionally she has facilitated numerous training sessions in several Caribbean countries including Belize and St. Lucia.

Dorcas is the proud mother of one son, David Allens who keeps her extremely busy. She can be reached via e-mail at projectmanagementsolutionsltd@gmail.com.

Resources

Andrews, D.H., and Goodson, L.A. 1980. "A comparative analysis of models of instructional design." *Journal of Instructional Development* 3(4):2–16.

Gagne, R. M *Principles of Instructional Design*. Forth Worth, TX: Harcourt Brace Jovanovich, 1992.

Harless, J. H. 1987. "An analysis of front-end analysis." *The Best of Performance and Instruction* 26(2):7–9.

Heldman, K. *PMP Project Management Professional Exam Study Guide*, 4th ed. Wiley Publishing, Inc., 2007.

Kirkpatrick, D. L. "Techniques for Evaluating Training Programs." in D. L. Kirkpatrick, ed., *Evaluating Training Programs*. ASTD. Alexandria, VA, 1975.

Lawson, Karen. *Train-the-Trainer Facilitator's Guide*. San Francisco: Jossey-Bass/Pfeiffer, 1998.

McFarland, R. D., and Parker, R. *Expert Systems in Education and Training*. Englewood Cliffs, N.J: Educational Technology Publications, 1990.

Merrill, M. D., Li, Z., and Jones, M. K. 1990. "Limitations of first generation instructional design." *Educational Technology* 30 (1):7–11.

Phillips, J. J. *Handbook of Training Evaluation and Measurement Methods*, 2nd ed. Houston, TX: Gulf Publishing, 1991.

Phillips, J. J., ed. 1992. *In Action: Measuring Return on Investment*, vol.1, ASTD, Alexandria, VA, 1994. p.262.

Project Management Institute. *A Guide to the Project Management Body of Knowledge*: PMBOK Guide, 4th ed. Project Management Institute, 2008.

Trimm, P., and Jones, C. *Business Communication Getting Results*, 2nd ed. Prentice Hall, 1987.